WHAT
MATTERS
MOST

ALSO BY JAMES HOLLIS, PH.D.

Finding Meaning in the Second Half of Life
Why Good People Do Bad Things

WHAT
MATTERS
MOST

Living a More Considered Life

JAMES HOLLIS, PH.D.

GOTHAM
BOOKS

GOTHAM BOOKS
Published by Penguin Group (USA) Inc.
375 Hudson Street, New York, New York 10014, U.S.A.
Penguin Group (Canada), 90 Eglinton Avenue East, Suite 700, Toronto, Ontario M4P 2Y3,
Canada (a division of Pearson Penguin Canada Inc.) • Penguin Books Ltd, 80 Strand,
London WC2R 0RL, England • Penguin Ireland, 25 St Stephen's Green, Dublin 2, Ireland
(a division of Penguin Books Ltd) • Penguin Group (Australia), 250 Camberwell Road,
Camberwell, Victoria 3124, Australia (a division of Pearson Australia Group Pty Ltd) •
Penguin Books India Pvt Ltd, 11 Community Centre, Panchsheel Park, New Delhi - 110
017, India • Penguin Group (NZ), 67 Apollo Drive, Rosedale, North Shore 0632, New
Zealand (a division of Pearson New Zealand Ltd) • Penguin Books (South Africa) (Pty) Ltd,
24 Sturdee Avenue, Rosebank, Johannesburg 2196, South Africa

Penguin Books Ltd, Registered Offices: 80 Strand, London WC2R 0RL, England

Published by Gotham Books, a member of Penguin Group (USA) Inc.

First printing, January 2009
10 9 8 7 6 5 4 3 2 1

Copyright © 2009 by James Hollis
All rights reserved

Gotham Books and the skyscraper logo are trademarks of Penguin Group (USA) Inc.

LIBRARY OF CONGRESS CATALOGING-IN-PUBLICATION DATA
has been applied for.

ISBN 978-1-592-40420-9

Printed in the United States of America
Set in ITC Galliard with Cresci and Medici Display

For Jill,

For Taryn, Jonah, and Seah

And for the people of the Jung Center of Houston, Texas, and Saybrook Graduate School of San Francisco

And with my deep personal thanks to those with whom I am most privileged to be associated:

Liz Harrison, agent, friend, sine qua non

William Shinker, President and Publisher, Gotham Books

Lauren Marino, Executive Editor, Gotham Books

And most of all for Timothy James Hollis,
  (2/69–11/07),
  son and friend who made me laugh,
  challenged my imagination,
  with whom I walked the high country,
  and who is with me always. . . .

  "The sufferings are not explained,
  nor all the lessons in love,
  nor what beholds us in death—
  only song, over our land,
  blesses and celebrates."

    R. M. Rilke, "Sonnets to Orpheus, #19"

Contents

PREFACE:
WHAT MATTERS MOST

*W*hat Matters Most: Living a More Considered Life is an admittedly eccentric compilation for which I offer neither apology nor justification. It pretends to no completeness, and will undoubtedly stir in the reader many other ideas, notions, prejudices, and predilections that could also have been included. (Such further thoughts, additions, and objections will thereby prove much the richer as readers are summoned to consider *what matters most* for them.)

I will not rehearse the usual list of *what matters most*, namely: friends and family, love, honor, good work, reputation, and the like. Matters thus obvious seem to take care of themselves. Of course relationships matter, for without them we would never find the dialectical challenge of "the otherness of the other" that causes us to grow. But this book asks each of us to consider more thoughtfully the relationship we have to ourselves, for that is what we bring to the table in the sundry scenes of this serial we call our life. With William Blake, I conclude that our highest faculty is not reason, useful and necessary as that is, but the imagination. The problem with our lives is that the stunted vision that our complexes, conditioned attitudes, and adaptive reflexes repeat lacks imagination. That is why our psyche protests and we are summoned to reconsideration by our symptoms.

Most of us would further agree that it matters that we bring no harm, or at least less harm, to others. This noble desire asks that we become progressively aware of, explore, take responsibility for our personal shadow. The shadow includes those parts of ourselves that make us uncomfortable with ourselves, whether it be our capacity for evil; our insurgent, narcissistic agendas; or our most spontaneous, healing, instinctually grounded selves.

There are many other ideas that are worthy of inclusion here in *What Matters Most*, but, because of space, they need wait another day. Among such a potentially infinite list are the following seven:

1. Life is a series of gains, but it is also a series of losses; *failures to grieve* loss and disappointment openly, honestly, will rise again, as unbidden ghosts from their untimely burial, through depression, or as projections onto objects of compelling, delusive desire, or through captivation by the mindless distractions of our time. Failure to incorporate loss into our lives means that we have not yet accepted the full package life brings to us. Everything given is also lost, redeemed by us only through a more conscious affirmation of values that we continue to serve.*

---

* In the midst of writing this book, I lost my beloved son, as have many other patients and parents. The sentences above were written long before. I can either curl up and die from grief, or live forward the values he and I shared. Jung challenges us directly: "Real liberation comes not from glossing over or repressing painful states of feeling, but only from experiencing them to the full." (*CW, 9i*, para. 587.)

2. The *recovery of personal authority* is critical to the conduct and reconstruction of the second half of life. If we are little more than our adaptations, then we collude with happenstance, and remain prisoners of fate. No matter how sovereign we believe we are, we remain the lowliest of serfs to the tyrannies of whatever remains unconscious.

3. Despite how risky love is, how easily we are hurt, none of us can run from *risking the dangerous shoals of love, compassion, and openness* to others, lest we live a sterile, unrelated life, locked within the constricted frames of our history and our comfort zones. The paradox of relationship will always be that rather than solve our problems for us, relationship brings us new problems, new complexities, but that we also grow immensely from these problems, these complexities. In short, the greatest gift of relationship proves to be that as the result of encountering each other, we are obliged to grow larger than we had planned.

4. All of us feel shamed by life; all of us consider ourselves failures of some kind, screw-ups in some arena important to us. Notice how *shame*, consciously or unconsciously, pulls us away from risk, ratifies our negative sense of worth through self-sabotage, or compels us into frenetic efforts at overcompensation, grandiosity, or yearning for validation that never comes. How much each of us needs to remember theologian Paul Tillich's definition of *grace* as accepting the fact that we are accepted, despite the fact that we are unacceptable.

5. Staying *psychologically balanced* so that in the good moments, we also remember the decline and dissolution that rushes toward us like tomorrow, *and* that in the moments of quiet despair we remember we have a soul, and that our soul is inviolate unless we give it away.

6. No matter how well intended we begin, sooner or later we all spend good portions of this journey stumbling through savannas of suffering, wherein we nonetheless find tasks that, when addressed—even in those dismal, diminishing circumstances—enlarge us. Going *through* suffering, rather than denying or anesthetizing it, knowing that if we hang in there, it will bring us choices that can either enlarge us or diminish us, and that when we are least in control, we still retain the freedom of choosing what matters to us.

7. And it matters *that we retain a sense of humor*. Humor is a way in which we honor the contradictions, acknowledge the discrepancies, suffer the reversals, and release the tension through laughter when, on other occasions, tears are our preferred recourse. Recall Robert Frost's wry couplet "Forgive O Lord my little joke on me / And I'll forgive Thy great big joke on me." In my desk I have two cartoons to which I frequently refer to keep things in perspective. One shows an analyst being asked what terms like *individuation* mean, and he says, "I haven't the foggiest. . . ." The other one shows a therapist being asked if he had cured anyone that day. "Not to my knowledge," he replies.

For some compelling reason, my mind is presently occupied by the story of the guy who takes his car to the mechanic. When he arrives to reclaim the vehicle, the mechanic says to him, "I couldn't fix your brakes, but I made your horn louder!" Does not this joke summarize our existential dilemma—at which we might as well laugh as cry: "Make do the best you can, patch it over, carry on. We can't fix your problem, but we urge you to honk on to the best of your ability."

Thus, the compilation of reflections that survives in this volume is designed to stir thought in the reader, possibly to reorient directions, priorities, and values. I have no vested interest in our becoming saner, or mentally balanced, or even useful to society. If you, the reader, find a neurosis that works for you, and gifts others as a bonus, then ride it for all it's worth. We are not here to fit in, be well balanced, or provide exempla for others. *We are here to be eccentric, different, perhaps strange, perhaps merely to add our small piece, our little clunky, chunky selves, to the great mosaic of being.* As the gods intended, we are here to become more and more ourselves. We, too, must enjoy amazement at what unfolds from within us while our multiplicitous selves continue to incarnate in the world, contribute, and confound.

I do not seek the reader's concurrence with my list, or with my conclusions, but I do ask that you reflect on your own life and come up with a list of your own. It may well prove that as we speak the truths of our own lives, we will also speak to the lives of others. In so doing, we find that the invisible community in which most of us participate is in fact *a community of exiles.*

We are all exiles, whether we know it or not, for who among us feels truly, vitally linked to the four great orders of mystery: the cosmos, nature, the tribe, and self? As a Western civilization we have not been affectively connected to these critical arenas of engagement since early in the fourteenth century, the time of Dante's marvelous picture of a three-storied universe, a world of moral cause/effect/ consequence, and of sacred/secular institutions providing perceptible longitudes and latitudes of the soul. Since that hour, much has unraveled, leaving us with disconnection, estrangement, and exile as our common lot. Yes, there are multitudes of people running about and shouting the Truth, that is, their fractal purchase on subjective prejudice, but their agitation betrays an old confession that *fervor is a defense against doubt*, and doubt is experienced as an enemy to be suppressed. Deeply driven by the need to suppress doubt, ambiguity, and ambivalence, they fall into sundry fervors, fevers, fears, and fundamentalisms. Such folk will surely find fault with the troubling reflections herein.

So, then, this book is written most for those who suspect that they are in fact exiles. Because of the erosion of the mythically connecting links to those four orders of mystery, the modern is driven to look within, to treasure personal reflection, to recover personal authority in order to find a creative path through the thicket of our time. When the world was still charged with the grandeur of the archaic gods, or when the institutional powers of mace and miter were still efficacious, one did not need to reflect. One lived the myth. When one experiences linkage to the numinous, one swims in it and serves it spontaneously. When we feel disconnected from the numinous, we either try anxiously to revivify the old linkage, drift off into the blandishments and distractions of popular culture, or suffer a crisis of meaning and are driven inward—whether to neurosis or privately encountered meaning remains to be seen.

As C. G. Jung observed, modern depth psychology was necessitated by the eclipse of tribal mythology. Presently, we are forced to look inward from whence powerful symbols emerge still, just as they appeared historically to the tribe, the shamans, and the prophets. The rule seems to be this: *When the gods are not experienced as living, felt force fields of energy, then we will project them outward and risk being owned by such numinous objects of our desire, or we will internalize them as somatic disorder or psychopathology.* Our own dynamic depths generate questions, images, and movements, whether we track them or not, respect them or not. As Jung observed in his memoir, *Memories, Dreams, Reflections,* life addresses questions to us, and we ourselves are a question. If we fail to observe, and engage in some form of cogent dialogue with the questions that emerge from our depths, then they, and our ill-considered, provisional answers, will continue to operate autonomously, and we will live an unconscious, unreflective, accidental life. So, then . . . let us reflect together for a while, consider what matters, what really matters, and then, in our wonderfully separate ways, fare forward together.

> *Fare forward, travelers! Not escaping from the past*
> *Into indifferent lives, or into any future. . . .*
> *Not to fare well,*
> *But fare forward, voyagers.**

James Hollis
Houston, Texas
2008

---

* T. S. Eliot, "The Dry Salvages," from *Four Quartets.*

"We have left land and taken to our ship! We have burned our bridges—more, we have burned our land behind us! Now, little ship, take care! The ocean lies all around you; true, it is not always roaring, and sometimes it lies there as if it were silken and golden, and a gentle favorable dream. But there will be times when you will know that it is infinite and that there is nothing more terrible than infinity. . . ."

FRIEDRICH NIETZSCHE, *THE GAY SCIENCE*

"Man's worst sin is unconsciousness, but it is indulged in with the greatest piety, even among those who should serve mankind as teachers and examples."

C. G. JUNG, *THE ARCHETYPES AND THE COLLECTIVE UNCONSCIOUS*

Chapter One

SHOCK AND AWE: THAT LIFE NOT BE GOVERNED BY FEAR

"Nothing in life is to be feared. It is only to be understood."
    MADAME CURIE

"Fear not.
What is not real,
never was
and never will be.
What is real,
always was
and cannot
be destroyed."
    THE BHAGAVAD GITA

"It is a bewildering thing in human life that the thing that causes
the greatest fear is the source of the greatest wisdom."
    C. G. JUNG

Something wakes you at three in the morning—a forgotten face reappears in a dream, a familiar apprehension stirs slumber, some ache agitates the soul. Or, driving on the expressway, hurrying home, a moment long ago leaks through psyche's floorboard into consciousness, and you wonder why it came to the surface just now, in this quite different place. You see your child, or grandchild, and recall a moment like that, and wonder where it all got lost, and how it all led to this place you are now obliged to call your life. You wonder how you became the person you think you are. How is it that you married the person you married? How is it that familiar doubts, self-sabotaging behaviors, predictable outcomes still govern your choices? Who is writing your as yet uncompleted biography—you, someone else, or unnamed sinister agencies? Just how is it that you got to this place, so different from the beginning of the journey, and how do you get back to where you lost your track amid the blizzard of necessary choices?

◆　◆　◆

Mewling and bawling, we were all flung into this world, expelled from the earlier place—our home, solace, respite—and, being thus bound to a perilous journey, end in extinction. "Astride of a grave," Samuel Beckett wrote, "with a forceps," coming or going, it is a rocketing, ratcheting, bracketing birth/death ride. Bewildered, traumatized, alone, we looked about and began to distinguish *this* from *that*, *me* from *not-me*, and thus the microscopic accretions of the promethean boon of consciousness—source of pain from knowledge of separation, privy to doubt, fear, and division, yet gift of awareness, ethical choice, and bright, necessary bauble of civilization.

Each of us, blood-bathed, shocked by light, gravity, cacophonous calamities, embark upon this fiercesome journey, fragile, frangible, and fearful. Batted about for decades—if the fates so decide—we recoil, make provisional sense of it all, and then succumb. Along the way we pass the time. . . . We ascribe our agendas to nature, create the gods, impugn their divinity through disregard, grind our brotherly and sisterly kind into dust and dismay, and create constructs, walls, clusters of folk, institutions, myths, diversions, speculations, programs, pogroms, and pass it all on to our spawn to play again. Sometimes, sitting on the side of a slope, we gaze at the stars and see patterns there, feel kinship with those twinkling, gaseous spheres racing farther from us by the millisecond, and register wonder, admiration, awe, a kind of joy, and forget, for a moment, the stupidities and brutalities of our lot. For a while, this monstrous, autophagous, engorging beast of daily life—the killing and eating, the being killed and eaten—is left behind, and wonder lifts us toward the larger. But most days we are simply stunned, stuporous, and frightened into compliant corners of being.

One African dawn, while on safari, Carl Jung slipped away from his tent and walked out into the veldt. He heard the sound of scavengers pursuing and eating their prey; he saw in the crepuscular dim great, gray streams of beasts sliding by before his astonished eyes. He knew that at that instant he had stepped from *chronos* to *kairos** and had entered a timeless moment. ("So it must have been, after the birth of the simple light," Dylan Thomas similarly mused in "Fern Hill," his moving account of his exit from the paradise of childhood wonder). The Swiss psychiatrist stepped out of

---

* As Kant pointed out two centuries ago, time exists solely as a construct of the mind, expressed in linear form, sequentially, as *chronos* and vertically, meaningfully, as *kairos.*

ordinary time and, for a moment, became the first human once again, staring on nascent brutish nature but bringing consciousness to it, recording it, observing it, conferring on it a reality (as Rilke also concluded)* it could never have achieved on its own. So in that moment the unique gifts of our transient tribe are celebrated: an endowment of recognition, a conference of consciousness upon brute being, and the grant of enhanced, reflective awareness.

Thus the gift our human tribe brings—upon such a slender branch on the great, ever-unfolding, evolutionary tree—but thus also the curse. That same consciousness that experiences joy, wonder, and devotion also suffers division, doubt, despair, ennui, enervation, and anxiety. Amid this tenebrific onslaught of life, consciousness forms around a tenuous telemetry of survival: what nurtures, feeds, supports, or comforts; what threatens, abandons, punishes, tempts, or tortures; what confounds with querulous quiddities and compelling conundrums? Slowly, this very vulnerability and adaptability winds its way around these mysteries and, befuddled, "reads" them carefully for clues, signs, suggestions, instructions, admonitions. It ponders, compares, contrasts, considers, internalizes, identifies, and "a provisional sense of self and world" evolves for each of us. In service to survival, and searching for sundry sensuous surfeits, it conjures up the illusion of permanence. Yet what, Goethe asked, provides *Dauer im Wechseln*, "permanence amid impermanence, continuity amid change?" What perforce provides consistency amid these perverse permutations? What

---

* In his ninth *Duino Elegy*, R. M. Rilke writes that this fleeting earth needs us, *we*, the most fleeting of all, to bring consciousness to brute being, to gift the vegetative *animal* sphere with *anima* or "soul."

but a necessary "fiction," the thought that *we* exist, that *we* are real, that *we* are permanent, and that *we* prevail.

But in every moment of certainty, every privileging of fractal consciousness, every necessary hubris, we also know something else! We know that we float above an abyss in every hour. As Pascal noted in his *Pensées*, the universe need not arm itself to destroy us. A drop of vapor will do, and if such viral velleities fail, there is always some molecular anomaly, the cancer of life multiplying so fast it eats flesh, blood, and bone. This roiling Angst that covers the highway we traverse with a perverse fog contains within it many possible fears, and in time our life is not only adapted to but governed by those fears, and our defenses against them. Thus, creatures who value life are pulled from it, collude against it, and destroy what they most desire. Desiring life, we deny death; denying death, we run from life!

So the child "reads" the world: the nuances, the intimations, and internalizes the direct and indirect "instructions." So the child "interprets" the world. So we arrive at this ever new moment with only interpretations, most deriving from a disempowered past. He or she concludes, in the hazy, mazy thinking of our beginnings: "What the world is, or does, or says, or fails to be, do, or say, is about *me*. It is all an elaborate message to me about *me*." So poverty of purse or spirit is extrapolated, construing a world of deprivation. So a preoccupied parent is interpreted as she or he who will not, does not, now or ever, value me as I am, and so I must slink off into the corners of the stage, or twist myself into feats that, attention-getting at last, cause them to regard me with approval. So the complexes, manias, agendas, desires, patterns, solicitations of those vital others are institutionalized within as operative definitions of ourselves through which we confirm, correct, or compensate the rest of our life. So it is that we read, misread, the world, transforming the fortuitous "out there" to a perduring "in here." In short, we all transfer the irruptions of the past into the conduct of daily life; we all suffer the fallacy of overgeneralization—what was true then, or apparently true, is repeatedly ratified, reinforced by what is reexperienced—and unwittingly re-created in each new venue.

◆ ◆ ◆

Brenda is driven, harried by unknown ghosts. Fearful, distrustful, she queries her husband continuously. Roger, compliant, guilty of nothing, begins to feel guilty for being himself, and then acts as if guilty. Soon they are in familiar roles: stern matriarch; cowed, furtive child. Each is playing out an archaic drama. Brenda was repeatedly lied to, deceived, disregarded by her narcissistic, immature parents. She now looks for betrayal, abandonment everywhere. After all, who could she ever really trust in this world if not them? Roger was the child of a salesman father who was always on the road, and a mother who promoted him to be her emotional companion. Each night he had to comb her hair, massage her neck, her back. Her unmet relational and erotic needs were naturally invasive to Roger, and yet, what was he to do, move away? Find another family?

Somehow, as it almost always seems to happen, Brenda and Roger find each other and play out this familiar drama. Brenda's constant, anxious scrutiny forces Roger to go underground, hide out, if only to protect the fragile soul within; his silences, systemic avoidances activate the archaic script

authored by Brenda's fate, through which she enacts the
same old, same old. Frustrated, unhappy, they come to therapy as a last resort. He feels harassed and guilty for being
who he is; she feels he is unreliable and evasive. Which one of
them is right, and who is writing this script? And how might
the iron bonds of such a compelling script be broken, and
different outcomes possible?

Each is acting "logically," given the emotional premise
embodied in their respective matrices of "self and other"
provided by the capricious gods of their contingent histories.
Brenda was terribly "betrayed," abandoned, by her intimate
others; Roger was terribly "invaded" by his intimate others.
Even though they are perfectly competent, well-intended,
productive adults, why would they not serve this archaic
programming and the carefully assembled reflexive responses
driven by their fears?

The presence of such programming came not as a surprise to these conscious adults, but the power of its pervasive influence from the unconscious was wholly unappreciated
until uncovered in therapy. Then came the taxing task of
sorting through these archaic images, separating them from
each other, learning to define anew what kind of relationship might prove worthy of two intentional adults, and what
consistent behaviors might lead in that direction. In recon-
structing their marriage, they were first asked to deconstruct
their own histories, and to dismantle the protective mechanisms that attended. Easier said than done. This work takes
years, not a single session, nor even a single season. Meanwhile, during this deconstruction/reconstruction, their
fragile commitment remains so tenuous, so vulnerable to the
imperatives and programs of the past. For the relationship to

survive, each must grant forgiveness and grace to the other, and hold steady in the presence of uncertainty for a considerable time.

◆ ◆ ◆

Given our fragile purchase on the world, given our obdurate dependency, given ignorance of alternatives, given the lack of rational analysis, given the imposing immensity of messages, we all assemble a false "sense of self." Not *false* because we have lied, but false because it is not about us, but about "them," about "it," about the "other." So we are defined by the other, not from within, not by divine design, but by "the otherness of the other," which we cannot fathom, understand, contain, control, comprehend. So we are defined as *a reticulated network of behaviors, attitudes toward self and world, and reflexive stratagems designed to get our needs met and to manage the anxiety in whose slipstream we daily stride.*

As most of this assemblage we call *ourselves* remains unconscious, we cannot usually address it, at least not until it becomes conscious. The fractious paradox of the unconscious is that it is unconscious! Yet some of us learn that there is such a thing as our *psyche*, a Greek word meaning *soul*. The psyche embodies the totality of our being: brain, blood, bone, cerebration, affect, and desire. It is who we are, though we can only know ourselves partially through the limited purview of consciousness. Yet it knows us, minds us, cares for us, corrects us, and critiques us when we are off track. It never sleeps, never ceases, always stands watch over our troubled slumber, and always registers its opinion as to how things are going.

When, from psyche's purview, things are going as they

should, when we are in the *Tao*, it provides us with energy sufficient for the task and supportive feeling that affirms the agenda. When we are off track, psyche protests. Noisy demonstrations are held in the amphitheater of the body; streets are blocked in the brain by rebels from the cane fields; dreams are invaded by spectral disturbances; affects riot and tear down the work of years. Meanwhile, the timorous ego, Nervous Nellie of Necessity, runs from these tumults, represses, splits off, projects, procrastinates, rationalizes, diverts, narcotizes, but the insurgents dig in for the long haul. "Our" abdication, our overthrow, seems their aim, and our terrors multiply. Whatever shaky throne we purchased at the price of numerous adjustments and backroom deals is our presumptive treasure and our sanctum. Nellie on the throne admits no faults, no threnodies for her reign, and simply orders more troops to guard the castle walls. The sundered sovereign, ego, will resist until resistance is futile: depression debilitates, the spouse leaves, the cost of the addiction is too much, troubling dreams persist, until a deep, shaming sense of sham may no longer plausibly be denied.

Thus psyche speaks, not with tongues of angels, but with sounding brass, and battens our brain and pummels our person till we collapse and open the door. Then begins the healing; then begins the recovery of what was lost by the necessary adaptations; then begins the wisdom of asking what *really matters most*.

Slowly, we begin to realize that for all the problems we face, the greatest problem is that we made many of them for ourselves. We begin to encounter the Zen-like wisdom that *what we have become is now our chief obstacle*. Those obligatory adaptations in the face of the twin threats to being—overwhelmment and abandonment—are now become a regnant, tyrannous government. Our adaptations make the decisions for us. While necessary to defend the child, they persist as autonomous directors of daily decision. Nervous Nellie, the timorous ego, is naturally identified with the party in power at any given moment. She easily becomes a ready bystander at a calamity, a passive observer at a funeral, a quisling in the parliament, a forlorn, sluttish companion to whomever offers her bread, sugar, comfort, and delusory surcease. Easily bought, she is a price heavy to bear by the soul.

If the autonomous psyche, or one's spouse or children, or the court, or some undeniable claimant did not beat on Nellie's door, she would never answer to what arrives on her front porch. But these presences crowd in upon her and demand recognition. So, humbled, perhaps shamed, and defeated, she enters therapy, attends a Twelve Step program, begins to pay attention to dreams, starts listening to the still small voice of psyche, a voice she knew well as a child, but relinquished in the face of the demands of the environment whose summons proved too imperious to ignore. So, Nellie may, through desperation, design, or defeat, learn how much her life is governed by fear, how much the whole blooming show she has become is driven by fear.

At first this recognition is shaming, demoralizing, but in the end it frees Nervous Nellie, for she learns that the fear that can be acknowledged, the fear that can be named, is no longer so monstrous. She finds that the fear will seldom in fact occur—although it might—and if it does, the adult world she inhabits, with its putative rationality, its freedom to make other choices, and most of all, its depth and resilience, allows her to survive, to push through, and to reclaim territory lost to the insurgents.

Learning that fear governs our lives, and the many coping strategies we have evolved to manage it, may be an unpleasant discovery, but it is the beginning of liberation. All it takes to recover the integrity of our journey is to recognize that fear is the enemy. Not others, not history, but plain old fear—*our* fears. As Jung observed, the spirit of evil is negation of the life force by fear. Only boldness can deliver us from fear, and if the risk is not taken, the meaning of life is violated.* That is pretty clear.

It is not the others on this planet who we should fear. After all, they are governed by fear as well. If we can remember that, then we will have less animosity toward them, and they will have less of a hold upon us. This does not mean that we need to be passive whenever they may be hurtful to us, but we are less likely to be caught in a repetitive, regressive cycle when we remember that fear is the common enemy. As I write, so many parts of the world are riven by fear, driven by animosity, and unable to see the frightened child in their enemies. We are governed by politicians whose survival as politicians depends on stoking those fears, and thereby dividing us from each other. We all seem to have forgotten the truth uttered by Philo of Alexandria millennia ago: "Be kind, for everyone you meet has a really big problem."

◆　◆　◆

While this emphasis upon fear seems reductionistic, perhaps simplistic, please remember that the most basic things, the things we hold in common, are what play the largest role in

---

* Cf. *Symbols of Transformation, CW 5*, Para. 551.

our lives. In the end, we all fear two things, two categories of existential vulnerability: the fear of overwhelmment and the fear of abandonment. Think of Brenda and Roger in the paragraphs above. She is driven by the terror of abandonment, that he will not be there in the end for her, and how can he be, really, given the magnitude of her need? He flees the horror of engulfment, and projects the devouring mother onto her. (I have written extensively on this subject elsewhere, but suffice to say, either threat begets elemental defensive strategies from each of us.)*

In the face of *overwhelmment*, which we feel from the earliest moments of our life, the core message is: "The world is big and you are not; the world is powerful and you are not; now, deal with that!" In response, we all develop patterns of avoidance, we succumb to the power complex, or we wind up accommodating what we perceive to be the will of the Other. In all the permutations of these forms, we are driven by fear, and over time we identify who we are with those protective devices. We practice them on a daily basis until we become them, or think we are.

In the face of the threat of *abandonment*, we evolve coping strategies that range from avoidance, gaining control over the Other, or inordinate searches for connection and reassurance. In the face of these core "ideas," we develop compensating behaviors ranging from self-sabotage, to narcissistic domination of others, to dependency patterns. And who among us can honestly say that we are immune to these threats, and who can profess to transcend these strategies of

---

* See *Finding Meaning in the Second Half of Life: How to Finally, Really Grow Up*, pp. 46–64

adaptation and survival? No wonder our psyche protests when it is overridden by fear-driven strategies rather than by a healthy connection to the instinctual truths and the developmental desires that lie at the heart of our being.

So there you have it. Fear is the enemy. Life is not your enemy; the Other is not your enemy; fear is the enemy, and fear has crowded you into a diminished corridor of that vast mansion of possibility that the gods provide us. Ask yourself of every dilemma, every choice, every relationship, every commitment, or every failure to commit, "Does this choice diminish me, or enlarge me?" Do not ask this question if you are afraid to find the answer. You might be afraid of what your own soul will require of you, but at least you then know your marching orders.

Only the boldest among us can acknowledge the role that fear plays in their lives. The bold are like those captives freed from Plato's cave—they are no longer servants to ignorance. If you are governed by fear—and who is not—and if you can acknowledge what it does to you, what it costs you and others for whom you care, and even the world to which you owe your best being, then you at last know, really know, to whom your final obligation belongs.

If you are still afraid, imagine your tombstone: "Here lies one who was not here, one who did not show up!" That is something to really fear; compared to this, our daily fears are trivial.

Every day, dual demons show up to make us miserable. One is fear, as we have seen, and the other is lethargy, a sweet, sibilant, seductive, susurrus that summons us to sleep. How easy to fall back into the sleep of innocence, naïveté, fundamentalism of one kind or another, avoidance, rationalization, and self-deception. These demons are the enemy of life.

Yet nature has provided us with an energy greater than these intimidating and seductive beasts, if we but call upon it. What we call "the archetype of the hero" is the specific constellation of energy whose task is the overthrow of darkness. When we see, for example, images of St. George and the dragon, what is he fighting? How many dragons have you seen? What is a dragon? A dragon is an archetypal, universal image representing the devouring fearfulness of life—that which would destroy you, or swallow you, or take you back to the cave. Sound familiar? Fear, and lethargy! So, the hero energy in you is nature's answer to the diminution and extinction of life. We are called to fight the dragon, slay its power. The dragon shows up every day, no worse for the wear, and ready to scare you back into a corner of your life, to swallow you, and to annihilate the life energy you are supposed to incarnate in this world. Whatever we are running from will sooner or later back us into the corner anyway. Sometimes, the things we fear show up in the flurry and flux of daily life, and sometimes at the hour of the wolf when we awaken to discover that not even sleep helps us hide. As poet Fleur Adcock expressed it:

> It is 5 A.M. All the worse things come stalking in
> And stand icily about the bed looking worse and worse
>   and worse.*

So, then, now you know your task: to become what the gods want, not what your parents want, not what your tribe

* Adcock, "Things," *Poems: 1960–2000.*

wants, but what the gods want, and what your psyche will support if consciousness so directs. A person who can undertake a conscientious inventory will be stunned to learn how much his or her life is driven by fear, as well as the many devices we evolve to manage it. Such a person then knows, really knows, what his or her life asks. The meaning of our life will be found precisely *in our capacity to achieve as much of it as is possible beyond those bounds fear would set for us.* There is no blame in being fearful; it is our common lot, our common susceptibility. But it may be a crime, an impiety against the gods, when our individual summons, our destiny, is diverted or destroyed by fear. For those of us who can address this inventory, our mantra, summons, and daily discipline becomes: *That Life Not Be Governed by Fear.*

Chapter Two

SAVING THE APPEARANCES: THAT WE LEARN TO TOLERATE AMBIGUITY

"We don't know a millionth of one percent about anything."
THOMAS EDISON

"I would never die for my beliefs because I might be wrong."
BERTRAND RUSSELL

"All great truths begin as blasphemies."
GEORGE BERNARD SHAW

Our conscious lives are driven by "pictures" and their attendant "stories." Some of these are quite conscious to us—*get a job, establish a relationship, look both ways before you cross the street,* and so on. Many more are unconscious—*do not be who you are for that is not safe, choose security over honesty, relinquish your personal authority lest it isolate you from others.* All of these messages, pictures, and stories are *complexes,* namely, energy-charged clusters of our history. We have complexes *because* we have histories, and history has an extraordinary power to write our biographies, frame our futures, circumscribe our freedoms.*

When we are caught between competing pictures, that is, pictures, stories, and messages that have directives critical to our being, yet are contradictory, we suffer crises of identity, crises of meaning. For example, when we were pushed out of the home and sent to kindergarten, we experienced colliding messages. "You are protected here, fed, relatively safe; now you must leave this secure place and deal with strangers, expectations generated by others, and many competing interests. Now you must leave here, this haven, forever!" The day I went to kindergarten, most of the children were crying. I did not know why. Now I do. Or remember the miseries of the adolescent passage, trapped as one is in an anarchic, insurgent adult body yet governed by the understandings and psychology of a child—another discordant set of pictures with contradictory messages. So too is the proverbial midlife crisis; so too is aging, loss, infirmity, the encounter with death, or any life nexus with confusing instructions, and subsequent crises of identity. What they all have in common is the disorienting experience of finding oneself in a limnal state. (*Limnos* is Greek for "threshold," and a limnal state is thereby a transition between two worlds.)

We continually walk between worlds—*this* conscious, tangible world, and *another* of which we are generally unaware. We are brought to the realization of their conjoined

---

* Another way to understand *complexes* was expressed by nineteenth-century Norwegian playwright Ibsen through the metaphor of "ghosts." In Act II of *Ghosts*, he writes, "It's not only what we have inherited from our father and mother that walks in us. It's all sorts of dead ideas, and lifeless old beliefs, and so forth. They have no vitality, but they cling to us all the same, and we can't get rid of them."

presence only when they are profoundly discordant. Look out the office window and observe the people passing many floors below. They traverse a tangible world, in service to ego-oriented goals, but in what compelling energies, scripts, archaic dramas are they really swimming? Can we tell from outside? Do they ever stop and examine what drives them? Could we ever claim to know them when we know next to nothing about the search engines that dictate their choices?

But our psyche always registers such discordant messages and overrules our ego—which believes it is in charge—by way of symptoms or troubling dreams, or even by prompting us to elect contrary choices that contradict our values or our self-interest. So, too, civilizations are often caught between "pictures," the "understandings" that once worked but which increasingly prove ineffectual. St. Augustine, for example, was driven to write *City of God* in the fourth century C.E. to help people psychologically absorb the ending of the stable world order as they had known it. Or, by killing 40 percent of all Europe in the fourteenth century, the Black Death seriously undermined the divine claims and eschatological pretensions of both monarchies and papacies. The Western world picture was shaken—the reverberations persist to this hour—and souls drifted into a profound disorientation, inadequately treated in time by the development of such secular surrogates as the modern welfare state, education, science and scientism, as well as seductive materialist comforts and diversions. Or, in our present moment, the putative fixity of definitions of race, gender, sexual preference or orientation, Western hegemony, trust in government probity, and many other presumptive truisms have been challenged, and largely overthrown, although many millions cling to the slope side of history in service to their psychological security. As a species, we ill tolerate ambiguity, contradiction, or whatever proves uncomfortable, and that is what makes the anxiety-fueled "fundamentalist" in each of us take over from time to time. When that nervous part prevails, we violate the complexity of life, serve regressive strategies, narrow and diminish the journey life asks of us.

◆ ◆ ◆

As specific case examples, let us look at two illustrations—one historic, one very personal—as described by a fifty-year-old man in my practice this week.

First the former. I have a photo in my office of Giordano Bruno, a man of natural curiosity who was burned at the stake by the church in 1600 at the Campo de' Fiori (the Field of Flowers—how charming such a locale must be!). What was Bruno's crime? He dared to trust his experience! He had heard of the work of the Polish astronomer Copernicus, who also trusted his experience, and who, based on his empirical observations, described a heliocentric planetary system with our sun at the center, as opposed to the venerated geocentric model in which the earth holds preeminent position, while the other suns, stars, and planets whirl about in fealty to *our* presumptive importance. Today we know that a heliocentric system is not only more accurate, but, much more, that we are only a small part of a much, much bigger universe in which we are no longer the apex and centrum, as the church and its models proclaimed. Rather we are space travelers aboard a speck of dust in a vast, whirling complexity so immense that we can only begin to imagine metaphors to intimate this infinity and even less can we create models to depict it. Today one does not point "up there" to identify "heaven" because there is no "up there" any longer. There is only "out there . . ." or is it "not here," or is it "not within"? But, then, is there anything that cannot finally be tracked back to "within"? The Cheshire Cat of *Alice in Wonderland* had it right—a subtle smile, a knowing wink—better than all the tautological certainties of the nervous. Yet, in this vast gap between images, humble faith may yet find its proper place by sacrificing angst-generated "certainties" for radical respect for the mystery.

Bruno endorsed those Copernican observations and thereby attracted the ire of prelates who considered him a threat to their anthropocentric, "divinely driven" metaphor with humanity and "its church" at the center of God's "plan." The erosion of this ordered, hierarchical model threatened the celestial cartography and its theological program upon which the authoritarian claims of the prelates depended. As Shakespeare, at the same point in history, wrote in *Troilus and Cressida*, "Untune that string, and hark what discord follows." In other words, if all the details do not fit into the master plan, suppress the details, or pay the price by loss of authority! This is why Bruno burns, not in service to truth, but in service to preserving someone's status quo! How little these fearful theo-thugs considered the hubris, the arrogance implicit in their summaries of and the limitations they placed upon their God. How little they acknowledged or confessed their presumption by asserting that they could even begin to imagine the complexity of the wondrous world in which we abide, a world wrought by their Almighty.*

---

* We still have such theo-thugs among us, whether they are mullahs who oppress people for being what their Creator intended, or pontiffs who purge seminaries, churches, and faculties. What they all have in common is psychic, and therefore spiritual, immaturity, evidenced by an impoverished imagination and a low tolerance for ambiguity.

For some time, observers whom we call scientists today had witnessed discrepancies in the received pictures and earnestly sought to "save the appearances"—namely, to find a way to acknowledge these discrepant details and still subsume them in service to the older models. Finally, the split grew too wide, the tension too great, and objective observation and the truth of personal experience captured the brain and the heart of these pioneers. Concurrently, Galileo looked through the recently invented telescope and, in 1610, saw that Jupiter has moons revolving around it.* What could not be seen with the naked eye now revealed itself to the magnified vision; from that moment on Galileo knew that the crystalline shells upon which the planets are putatively pasted, and that revolve in celestial harmony, could not exist without those moons breaking them.** And he said so. Predictably, by 1610 Galileo was also threatened with torture by Robert Bellarmine—the same Inquisitor who burned Bruno—put under house arrest, and forbidden to publish his disturbing views.

Thus the fascist mind—which is always with us, in whatever culture, waiting to control what you or I might experience for ourselves. Why? *Because it makes them uncomfortable!* Today they show up on school boards and try to remove books that challenge their antiquarian, three-story universe. Today they seek to impose creationist dogma as science, in

---

* Within a year the moons were confirmed by Jesuit astronomers and by Kepler in Prague. They were named Io, Europa, Ganymede, and Callisto after a suggestion made by Kepler in 1613.

** Do you recall the old hymn that proclaims "All nature sings and around me rings, the music of the spheres"? Those spheres refer to the fantasy that the planets revolved in Divine harmony on transparent, crystalline spheres that, if one were spiritually attuned, could be heard as a celestial harmony.

the name of free inquiry, of course, despite the fact that no serious scholar of the Bible would assert that the poetic metaphors of Genesis were other than the creative imagining of a people who were not themselves present at the beginning. Thus, like the nervous prelates of Bruno's day, they deny the reality of evolutionary process even as their bodies mutate and evolve within their short lifetimes in reaction to antibiotics and environmental toxins. Thus, they serve as representatives to the U.S. Congress, and argue that another duly elected representative should not be sworn into office holding his sacred book.* Thus, they show up by labeling dissent, different views, and sincere questions as unpatriotic and disloyal. Thus, the fascist mentality occurs wherever ambiguity occurs. And thus, dear reader, there will always be someone perfectly willing to burn a Bruno—or you—if you differ! So much they want, need, to "save the appearances," deny the discrepancy, patch over contradiction, and make all things fall within their control.

❖　❖　❖

In my office recently, a fifty-five-year-old carpenter told of the time he was afflicted by a catastrophic illness. Local church worthies insisted that they hold an interventionary faith healing on his behalf. His passive, perhaps intimidated,

---

* As in the case of Representative Virgil Goode (R-VA), who was upset that a colleague, elected to office by the citizens of another state, came from another faith, and wished to prevent him from choosing the *Korán* as his holy book. Moreover, this guardian of the U.S. Constitution and its Bill of Rights, which guarantee freedom of thought and worship, urged voters to vote against any other Muslim lest they also make similar choices. Your tax dollars at work. . . .

parents agreed. The ceremony was duly held but his illness only progressed.

The night before the ceremony, this youth, thrust by fate into a strict religious sect, violated one of the precepts of his tribe. He nervously drank a beer. He never had before, but that evening he felt a deep desire to drink a beer. For many years he believed that drinking that beer had sabotaged the healing ceremony, offended God, and similarly the ecclesiastic worthies who had brought this business upon him. His physical burden was thus enhanced, doubled, by a spiritual burden of complicitous guilt.

In my office, reviewing this concatenation of events some four decades later, he suddenly realized why he'd had to have that beer. He had not really believed the ceremony would be efficacious! Even as a youth, he felt it was something coercive and even superstitious. So something in his unconscious committed this "offense" to *save God*. How would he save *God*? He was saving "the image of God" that he and his tribe espoused, and in which he so loyally wished to believe. Rather than blame God for the "failed" healing, he would take that burden upon himself. In other words, he was unwittingly trying to "save the appearances" and thereby enable the two stories within his soul to be reconciled.

While this event, and his "heroic mission," remained only dimly remembered for decades, his history has always been burdened by this alleged complicity. At the time, the faith healer, epigone of spiritual magnanimity, accused him of lacking in faith and told him that if he ever found sufficient faith, he would be healed of his affliction. How kind, how deeply imbued with the spirit of charity and healing spirit this worthy was! To the crippling affliction the youth suffered, he was now condemned to bear the weight of spiritual failure. So much for "saving the appearances," and so much for those moral stalwarts who remained ignorant of the virus that produced his polio.

So, these decades later, in a moment of therapeutic insight, he recalled the beer the night before, and together we recognized that what he did was sacrifice himself to save "God," that is, the *imago Dei* of his sect. He had offered himself up, the willing child, to be tortured in service to God. *Hoc est corpus meum.* He proved a Christ-like surrogate sufferer so that he could "save the appearances" for himself at that stage of his youthful journey, and for his tribe as well. His "offense," then, is what is oxymoronically called a "holy crime," an act that violates the culture-bound, normative rules, but in service to a higher goal. Do we not notice the parallel between the spiritual worthies who burned Bruno and those who savaged this child—all in service to their need to treat the anxiety that rises from ambiguity?

◆　◆　◆

This tendency to "save the appearances" shows up in all our lives when we manage to dissemble, to deny, to lie to ourselves and believe our evasions. We are often called to save the appearances, to paper over the gap between our presumptive identity and values and our actual practices. This distressing gap is what Jung called the *Shadow*, those parts of ourselves that make us uncomfortable with ourselves. Feeling discomfort, we repress these facts, project them onto others, are subsumed by them, or, occasionally, bring them to consciousness and integrate them into a more complex, more accurate sense of self.*

Protecting our persona, deflecting responsibility for our choices and their consequences, fitting in with collective values—all are means by which we seek to "save the appearances" and avoid the discomfort of ambiguity.

The truth is, all of life is a grand, blooming ambiguity. The more we know about it, the more we realize we do not know. Two and a half millennia ago Socrates was identified by the Delphic oracle as the wisest man in all of Greece. Knowing himself well, Socrates thought such a proclamation preposterous. So he traveled about his land and sought out resident wise men and women, whom he found to be unwittingly ignorant, at best, and self-deluded. In time he came to understand that his wisdom was that he knew that he did not know. And he was strong enough in character to accept this fact, and thereby earned his "wisdom."

Our maturational process is directly linked to the capacity to progressively handle ambiguity, discomfiting as it may prove. In fact, the test of psychological, political, social, and spiritual maturity is found precisely in the capacity of any person to tolerate ambiguity. Yet, if we are honest and observant, there is a fascist within each of us, a Nervous Nellie who wishes comfort at any cost. As Hannah Arendt wrote in *Crises of the Republic*, throughout history the totalitarian mind is obsessed by a need for the world to be clear-cut and orderly. Accordingly, subtleties, contradictions, and complexities are felt as intolerable, and have to be eliminated by

---

* For a fuller discussion of the theme of the Shadow, please see my recent *Why Good People Do Bad Things: Understanding Our Darker Selves*.

whatever means. Such a nervous tyrant lives within each of us, and may rise up at any provocation to stifle dissent, or crush the alternative that wishes to come into life through us. Just as we live within haunted houses, so we live as vassals in a tyrannous state.

The efficacy of a democracy certainly depends on opposition, for any one-sidedness proves totalitarian quickly. The maturity and differentiated capacity of our personality depends on respecting ambiguity, without which we would never grow, never question, never move out of the old certainties that once offered comfort, but in time only *ratify ignorance and oblige constriction.* An ability to tolerate the anxiety generated by ambiguity is what allows us to respect, engage, and grow from our repeated, daily encounters with the essential mysteries of life. But the payoff goes even further. Certainty begets stagnation, but ambiguity pulls us deeper into life. Unchallenged conviction begets rigidity, which begets regression; but ambiguity opens us to discovery, complexity, and therefore growth. The health of our culture, and the magnitude of our personal journeys, require that we learn to tolerate ambiguity, in service to a larger life.

◆ ◆ ◆

One further thought on all this. Our personal psychologies, our theologies, our politics are chiefly designed to make *us* feel more comfortable, more secure. This is not a federal offense, for fear is an inescapable aspect of our journey; however, these constructed forms favor our comfort more than they serve "the gods"; they are our efforts to make deals with truth, in whatever protean and challenging forms it may appear. But in the end, the gods will not be mocked, the truth will out, and our flights from ambiguity will lead us, and our culture, to dead ends: spent ideologies, failed theologies, and trivializing psychologies. Is it acceptable that our lives end governed by fear, by flight, and by triviality—all in the face of the immensity of ambiguity in which we in fact swim at all times? Is it possible that rather than try to "save the appearances"—namely, paper over discrepancies between theory and fact, between model and mystery—we embrace the unknown? Would not that prove more honest, more faithful, more respectful, less fear-driven, less diminishing, less trivializing of the depth and majesty of this universe and our transit through it?

Chapter Three

STARVING AMID ABUNDANCE: THAT WE CONSIDER FEEDING THE SOUL

> *"[Fanaticism is] redoubling your efforts where you have forgotten your aim."*
>
> GEORGE SANTAYANA

*T*hese first sentences are written on December 22, while the feeding frenzy of mawkish mercantilism is in full fury. People are storming the Internet, slowing search engines to a crawl. They are pushing one another in the crowded shopping centers. The major networks are nervously reporting sales figures as if they were tsunamis or plagues of locusts at our door. Admittedly, this day provides an opportunity for the observation of a major sociological event. I once took a professor colleague of mine to the 700 level of the old Veterans Stadium to watch the Philadelphia Eagles play. Perched on that nose-bleed eyrie we sat amidst a most raucous crowd, one for whom multisyllabic words were rare but beer abundant. My friend's discipline was anthropology, and if he saw 10 percent of the game, I would be surprised. He was fascinated by the native behaviors going on around him. For him, it was a sociological and anthropological event, and he thanked me for the field trip. So is the feeding frenzy of this hour. A foreign observer might think such folk as we see storming the stores are starving, and that those stores hold caches of food.

What is going on here? How is the Prince of Peace, the humble servant in the stable, being celebrated? How are his values being emulated, this man who said that his kingdom was not of this world? What are we to make of these frenzied solstitial rituals? At least millennia ago, when, in acts of sympathetic magic, our ancestors lit candles or created bonfires to entice the sun to return, something vital was at stake. They desperately hoped to nurse, cajole, seduce the sun to swing back from its great arc southward, lest they perish from the bitter cold and the crops fail to return for lack of the sun's seminal rays. Well, perhaps something vital *is* at stake here . . . still, even in all this shopping madness. Wheresoever such energy is invested, something vital must be at stake, but it may have little to do with Jesus, or what Yeats once called "the Galilean turbulence on the bestial floor."

◆　◆　◆

When we reflect upon the fact that annually tens of millions of tourists/pilgrims trek to the casinos of Atlantic City* and Las Vegas, then we are obliged to ask why.

Why do millions make this hajj, this mass migration toward admittedly secular cities? Why, like Chaucer's sojourners to Canterbury Cathedral, do they from every shire's end

---

* At last count the annual average number of tourists/pilgrims arriving in Mecca is three million plus, Disney World ten to twelve million, and Atlantic City and Las Vegas each more than thirty-three million per year.

their sundry pilgrimages wend to this dilapidated city by the Jersey shore, or that plastic artifice in the desert? It has to mean something!

Why do they come? Well . . . "Money," one replies. "What kind of fool are you to ask such an obvious question?" Well, what, then, *is* this money, that organizes so much of human energy? Why do they come? Really, why . . . ?

When we look closer, we see that they come not because of money, which after all is embodied by plastic discs, pieces of metal, or slips of paper. We may even admit that these glittering pleasure palaces, named to evoke medieval, antique, or sybaritic associations, are seductive. (Who might not want to see for oneself Caesar's palace, or the Taj Mahal, or the Tropicana, especially when they're only a bus ride away?) Seductive, too, are the green felt tables, the constant din, the sensory overload, the *ka-ching*, *ka-ching* of coin, the hint of sex and excitement, the thrill of play, risk, gain, and loss. But what, really, is it all about? Why are the poor, the elderly, the disadvantaged most likely to show up there, having gotten on a bus in Baltimore, boarded a free flight from Dayton or Richmond, or a waiting limo from LaGuardia? Why do the millions persist in such pilgrimages when the games are so obviously tilted in favor of the house? Why would I voluntarily, even enthusiastically, hand over my money, knowing full well that I am being manipulated by images, sounds, sights, temptations, decor, and deception? Why would I ignore the story of the young man, buried by the A.C. *Press* in the second section, who kills himself in the marshy reeds along the Black Horse Pike, knowing that he took his company's money and lost it all? Why would I want to support a company that flew its private jet to Montreal to bring a pathetic, addicted, low-level bank employee down to gamble and lose tens of thousands of someone else's money each weekend? Why would I want to turn my Social Security check over to the money moguls when the price of groceries in Fresno keeps rising? Why, knowing that the casino directorate does not love me, would I want to go give them the fruits of my often sad, onerous labors? Why would I want to put their children through college?

What will this putative money bring these pilgrims, besides new complications, tax problems, and escalated fantasies to go with an elevated blood pressure? What does money offer us, or rather, what do we offer money by the projections we place upon it? Projections are aspects of our unconscious, so we do not know that we have projected an aspect of the soul on such inanimate tokens. After all, if people can project their soul onto flags, oaths, institutions, causes, heroes, or celebrities, why not onto money?

When we untangle the complexity of our fantasies, we find that there are three substantive projections onto money, and can thereby access clues into the peculiar role that Atlantic City, and other such Xanadus, play for us.

1. The first is that if I win money—if I am gifted by fate, or by my own "talents," or visited by Lady Luck—I am lifted out of the ordinary. For the moment I leave this horizontal plane of my taxing, boring life and become extraordinary. For the moment, I *transcend*. In *The Fall*, Albert Camus describes how thrilling it proves when someone is murdered in the neighborhood. For a moment, then, a "transcendent" event, a distraction, lifts one out of the horizontal. Every night the local news begins with the latest murder, or horrendous wreck, or

salacious scandal. (A friend who is in the TV news business told me their mantra for the opening story is: "If it bleeds, it leads.") For a moment, then, the hope of apparent transcendence of the ordinary compels my devotion.

2. Secondly, I fantasize that with money I can *transform* my life, not just pay off the mortgage, but fill my life with new, distracting objects (which thereby come in time to own me). But, even more, I fantasize that these gifts will transform me and *I* will be different, better, more of something. Transformation promises that I can finally *become* . . . become more than I am, more than whatever I achieved on my own, more than what was given me, more than the fates hitherto permitted.

3. Thirdly, with money I can momentarily feel *connected to something larger* than me. I can experience awe, excitement, a relationship to the transcendent *Other.* I can feel part of something bigger, can reframe my life, step into magnification, feel again "connected," when so much of our lives we feel estranged, separated. My loneliness, my sorrow, my yearning are for the moment palliated by this momentary "connection."

Notice these values, these profound desires, agencies, agendas of our insistent soul: *transcendence, transformation, connection.* Those are "religious" values. The historic office of religion was to provide a sense of transcendence from tawdry daily life, to fundamentally transform it into something eternal, and to reconnect the separated soul to its source, which is what the etymology of *religion* means.*

If we find ourselves in a living mythological system, that

---

* Cf. "*re-legare.*"

is, where the energy-charged images of our tribe, family, or culture in fact change us, lift us, connect us, then something abstract, contrived, and trivial like money loses its charm. The debts of life are a pragmatic concern, and may be addressed in pragmatic ways, but money for the sake of money is spiritually irrelevant, affectively flat. Apparently, since we millions make this thing, this money, so urgently relevant, is it because we millions are not able to experience effective spiritual life somewhere else? Yes, churches are full—perhaps more than ever in America, though far less so in most of the rest of the Western world. Perhaps they are full because they are ready containers for the anxiety generated by the "grand disconnect" that has transpired since Dante's time. Groups flocking together at a mega-church or a casino have at least one ingredient in common, namely, a generalized existential angst that they are trying to treat by seeking reconnection, a promise that is seldom fulfilled in a sustained and sustaining way for most adherents of either altar. Perhaps the churches are so packed in America, and the casinos even more, because we are in fact so spiritually impoverished and our souls are so desperately hungry.

◆　◆　◆

If I am going to use a word like *soul*, perhaps I ought to try to define it. *Soul*, the literal translation of the Greek word *psyche*,* is inherently indefinable but is a word, a metaphor, to describe what we consider to be our essence. It is the energy

---

* *Psyche* has two etymological roots, or metaphoric origins: the verb "to breathe," and the "butterfly," a being that transforms mysteriously from dross matter to the beautiful and elusive.

that blows through us, that enters us at birth, animates* our journey, and then departs, wither we know not, at our passing. As the brain is the organ of thought, and the heart the organ of circulation, and the stomach the organ of digestion, so the "soul" is the organ of "meaning." When life is lived in accord with psyche's intent, we experience inner harmony, supportive energy, feeling confirmation, and we experience our lives as meaningful. When we, or the world, violate the intent of psyche, we suffer symptoms; we pathologize on personal or collective bases.**

If the images presented to us by our culture in fact fed the soul, we would not hunger so much. If they linked us to the divine realm, connected us in compelling ways to our tribe, or buttressed our spirits on this perilous journey, we would not be so hungry, would not have to turn to such trivializing pursuits as casinos and mega-churches, whose Sunday extravaganzas are more often choreographed show business than humbling engagement with the mystery of being.

We are the most affluent culture in history, the most gifted with material abundance, *and* we are starving. As T. S. Eliot once suggested, when global warming is done with us, when the dust rolls across our cities, our only monuments will be concrete highways and a thousand lost golf balls —expressive artifacts of a people always going somewhere because where they are is intolerable, soliciting as many distractions along the way as possible. Thus, we have reared up temples of both sacred and secular claim to

---

* The word *animates*, from the Latin *anima*, literally means to "en-soul."

** The word *psychopathology* literally means "expressing the suffering of a soul."

tempt and seduce us into feeling fed, though we continue to starve.

◆　◆　◆

In addition to the culture-driven complexes* that convince us our lives are better because they are more comfortable, we also are driven by whatever personal complexes our fate, our family of origin, our institutions have generated and reinforced. So many of us engage in pursuits of the symbolic, which our projections construe as salvation, or reinforce addictions to palliate our suffering, or find distractions to help us avoid our pain, or perform acts of self-destruction because we hate our lives so much. Set aside for a moment our trivializing popular culture, which imagines it has to create "reality" shows when so much of the world is really hurting; mindless excitations of the senses in ever-increasing intensity; and pseudo-dramas in which our perturbations of soul are worked out for real in high tragedy and base comedy every hour. We have so much turmoil within that, despite these many distractions, we are compelled to return to ourselves, to what Gerard Manley Hopkins called "our own sweating selves." Or Frost, considering the great empty spaces out there in the interstellar world, concluded that "I have it in me so much nearer home, / to scare myself with my own desert places."

Let us consider Jordan for a moment. Jordan is one of

---

* *Complexes* can be defined here as energized "ideas" that, mobilized, mobilize us in return. They have a point of view, a quantum of energy, and a mythological "screen" through which the world is construed, and they have an attending script that fosters a repetitious response to the ever-changing circumstances of life.

the truly fine, decent men who has given everything to his family, his tribe, and his city. When he could have retired and played golf with his neighbors, he went to work for his city for a dollar a year and devoted himself to helping the helpless in his city. When we began to consider his own needs, he replied that he could not begin to do so because, after all, there are so many children in Africa and Asia who are dying of disease and malnutrition, and indeed there are. How could one fault such a considerate man and his great ethical sympathies?

But Jordan is starving, and has always starved, and has not even known it—at least not until now. Jordan, like so many of us, has lived his life in service, not just to the family and city, but to the iron sovereignty of core complexes presented to him by fate. While his service to others has been exemplary, his own soul has starved in those "desert places." Child of a driven, domineering father who would accept nothing but the greatest of achievements from his children, Jordan got the clear message that his needs, his reality, were not just secondary but were unworthy of consideration. His assignment, imposed upon him by his father's neurosis, was to "get with the program." Accomplishing "the program" meant being successful in his business life, becoming a paragon of public virtue, and staying on top of all the tasks people would bring to him and expect him to solve for them.

But in all this mélange of messages, Jordan never felt permission to have his own life, or pursue the legitimate ends of his own desires. The psychology that dominated his childhood quite predictably ordained continuing self-sacrifice to a narcissistic wife for whom nothing was ever enough. Their children grew accustomed to demanding and manipulating their father. When he and his wife finally separated, he was vilified and lost the allegiance of his children whose bodies were adult, but whose attitudes had been programmed by their mother.

So, when we later hear Jordan saying that he can hardly imagine doing something for himself when there are so many so horribly in need, we need to see that this is not just compassion speaking, and generosity of heart—although it is that—but the replication of his long history of emotional starvation in the midst of plenty.

So when is a good thing a good thing, and when is a good thing not a good thing? To answer that question we have to track the very subtle wiring that leads from the decisions we make consciously back into our historic basements. A central psychological truth, then, is *it is not what we do, but rather what our action is in service to the unconscious that matters.* Jordan's good acts for others might well have risen from his generous heart. But when Jordan repeatedly, reflexively, defers his own interests in service to others, how is that not an enslavement to the organizing and determinative power of archaic complexes? The core message of his early conditioning was that his wishes did not matter, that the hierarchy of needs was generated by others, and that his well-being lay in proving continuously capable of taking care of others.

All of us are enslaved by organizing "ideas" derived from our history. These complexes are such constant companions that we have rationalized them thoroughly. We say, "Well, that is just the way I am," or "It is always that way," or "To get along you go along." Creatures of adaptation that we necessarily are, we also grow progressively estranged from that instinctual source Jung called the *Self*—to be distinguished from the beleaguered ego, a servant of so many compulsive, repetitive, reductive messages, yet deluded in thinking it is the CEO.

It is my clinical experience that most of us do not have abiding permission to fully claim our own lives. Sadly, this means that we are often living in a fragmented, partial way. Our soul—that is, our psyche—knows this of course, grieves, and presents us with those many protests we call symptoms.

In the case of Jordan, many of us see ourselves—our rationalized, conditioned, cooperative selves. The good news about Jordan is that he is now in a serious analysis, has come to recognize the immense cost of his early, coerced compliance, his collusion against his own soul, and has recently been making large choices about his work life, his relational life, his spiritual life, and his avocational life. Just today we concluded that this man in his sixties must review every commitment, every old friendship, every practice, and every summons, and say in a new way, "I will not serve that which does not serve me."* This is not self-aggrandizement, not narcissism; it is service to the soul. Finally, this man is learning to respect what he was called to be, on his own, minus the coercive instructions from his family of origin and the many similar admonitions that followed and repeated this psychologically divisive message. All of them, intentionally or not, exploited his captive will, and he colluded. At last

---

* This sentence echoes that of James Joyce's roman à clef, *Portrait of the Artist as a Young Man*, where Stephen Dedalus concludes that he must leave Ireland forever, for he can no longer serve the family, church, and the nationalistic ideologies that no longer serve him. After a life lived in exile in Paris, Trieste, and Zurich, Joyce's repayment to history remains the greatest works in English fiction in the last century.

Jordan is working on not starving while in the midst of plenty; having served others, he may finally begin to feed his own soul.

Maybe all of us stand to learn more about the recovery of our own soul from his new insight, and his new commitment. Maybe all of us will learn to grapple with the paradox that living our lives more fully is not narcissism, but service to the world when we bring a more fully achieved gift to the collective. We do not serve our children, our friends and partners, our society by living partial lives, and being secretly depressed and resentful. We serve the world by finding what feeds us, and, having been fed, then share our gift with others.

In his short story "A Hunger Artist," Franz Kafka depicts a man who becomes a circus act whose "performance" is simply fasting. For a while, he awes people; then they are bored and turn to more diverting side shows. When asked why he fasts, he replies that he would have eaten, had he found something that tasted good, something that truly fed his soul. This story is a sad parable of much of Kafka's personal suffering, but even more a powerful reminder to each of us that something within us wishes to be fed. It is the task of the considered life to honor that need and find what really feeds, what really summons growth, as well, and then share that larger expression of soul with others.

So, then, what feeds you, and how do you know? Some basic tests are available to us all, and their validation arises from our own psyche. There are no right answers—there are your answers, and other people's answers—to these tests. No one else can tell you what is right for you; at best they can attest to what is right for them, if they even know that. Those who are readily prepared to tell you what is right for you are not your friends. They are unconsciously seeking validation of their own tenuous choices through your compliance.

How often in therapy I hear people describe the fact that the values, or the venues, in which they have invested their resources no longer provide satisfaction, no longer energize. They find themselves forcing themselves to service what once seemed to make sense. One of the signs of the fact that the psyche moves on, whether we will it consciously or not, is the appearance of boredom, ennui, loss of energy. When we are doing what the psyche wants, the energy is there and the excitement is palpable.

Of course it can be argued that when we are in the full flush of a complex, such energy also supercharges our lives. But the key is to monitor the presence of energy, symbolizing the activated psyche, over time. This discernment, this sorting, requires paying attention to feeling states, to levels of satisfaction, to reciprocity. We experience the greatest richness in our lives when we invest in some task or value and it returns to us by way of satisfaction or meaning. In those moments of reciprocity we feel a resonance, a deep consonance. If we are doing what is wrong for us, we can will it up for a short time, and reality often requires that we do so; but over time, the psyche will abandon us, and the symptoms emerge.

As a therapist, I am a frequent attendant upon the fact that someone's symptoms are expressing a will contrary to their conscious intent or their complex-driven agendas. Healing, satisfaction, and meaning only come when we identify what feeds our soul, and find also the courage and the wherewithal to make it happen. I have been asked so often by a person at a perplexing crossroad, "Should I do this, or this?"

Often, I have answered, "Yes." That is, both paths embody values to that person, and he or she is thereby summoned to find the resolve, the energy, the ingenuity, the sacrifice, the courage to affirm both paths at the same time. Such a discerning person finds that the cost of such efforts to change proves far less than the cost of ignoring the hunger our soul brings us on a daily basis.

The soul is a hungry child at our door. How long can we ignore its presence?

Chapter Four

THAT WE RESPECT
THE POWER OF EROS

"Over his grave
the household of Impulse mourns one dearly loved:
sad is Eros, builder of cities,
and weeping anarchic Aphrodite."
"IN MEMORY OF SIGMUND FREUD," W. H. AUDEN

*W*e mostly wish to live orderly lives, predictable lives, controlled lives. Susan falls in love, is jilted, slices her wrists. Why? Is this any way to impress the next boyfriend? Arnold works like a slave, toadies up to everyone who can advance his career, finally achieves the corner office, the one with windows on both sides, and then, without explanation, walks away and is never seen again. Why? Where is he, and will he ever unlock to himself or others what so drove him? Thomas, a freshman at a university, learns his parents are divorcing. He affects nonchalance, *sangfroid*, but will not even tell his dates who he is, from whence he comes, and what he feels. Why? Is he so frightened of feeling again, that is, of feeling consciously what he already is feeling? Inexplicably to all her friends, Angela walks away from her marriage of twenty years. Safe, secure, valued by all, including her husband, she walks away. Why? When asked, she mumbles, "I wanted to know that I wasn't dead yet."

Each of these persons is gripped by an energy, a fever, a passion, a desire for something larger, and, frustrated, denied, misdirected, or betrayed, they plunge forth into troubled waters. Why? What drives them? What causes them such contradictions, such self-defeating moments, such urgency?

◆　◆　◆

Our ancestors venerated Eros as a god, variously described as the earliest of the gods, providing the root and fundament of all life forms, and the youngest of the gods, renewing itself in every unique moment. What is Eros, and how does It/He/She conform with or differ from the erotic? What is the proper role of this "god" in our lives? How, when all of us have had our hearts cracked and crazed, if not broken forever, can we still steer our leaky craft through the dangerous but necessary shoals of love? How can we honestly grieve loss and disappointment and still, with due deliberation, plunge again into risk and emotional danger? How can we, in the face of shame and failure, open to life, and open repeatedly? How can we honor Eros, this much misunderstood god, yet not be enslaved by It/Him/Her? Who among us has not made foolish, irretrievable decisions while possessed by this god? Who among us does not long for such violent possession? Who among us can control that god, or compel its acquiescence to our agenda? And why would we so eagerly return to get beat up again by such a petulant god, over and over again? Perhaps because we have no choice, because Eros is a god, and we are not. Eros drives us toward ends not our own at times, but in service to the fuller expression of the permutations of possibility.

◆　◆　◆

So, when we speak of Eros here, let us see him as our predecessors did, as a *god*. When we use the phrase *a god* here we are not making metaphysical or theological declarations at all. Rather the metaphors of *the gods* are useful constructs, ways of valuing, dramatic embodiments of the elemental energies of the universe, energies that have animated and driven life from the beginning and drive us all still today. They are the force fields that energize and move us toward their sundry ends beyond the powers of conscious comprehension, mythstreams in which we swim all the time. Why call them *gods?* Such a construct, such an expression, risks confusion with metaphysical reality, but herein the metaphor of *the gods* is simply meant to suggest immensity, endurance, significance, and our respectful acknowledgment of these large, transcendent energies that course through our histories.

Eros is the life force—*desire* that wishes most to connect, to build, to combine, to fuse, to generate with the other. Eros is an archetypal power whose necessary twin is *Logos*, the dividing, separating, differentiating energy. In our bodies, minds, souls, both energies are continuously manifest. The one wishes merging, connection; the other splits, divides, and diversifies. One energy without the other balancing it becomes not only one-sided but even demonic. (The *demonic* occurs whenever some value or force is expressed without its opposite, its countervalence, its contrary, also being respected. Even "good," expressed without constraint and consciousness, begets "evil" in time.)* What the

---

* In *Why Good People Do Bad Things*, I give multiple examples of how even the good can produce negative outcomes, how, paradoxically, the good can sometimes be the enemy of the better, and how our moral task is not goodness but wholeness.

gods most want of us is respect, mindfulness, and when we forget them—that is, the energies they embody—we create monsters, whether in our bodies, our ideas, or our social systems.

The protean power of Eros is present everywhere in daily life, in our conversations, our food, our creative acts, our copulation and procreation, our fantasies, and both our popular and our sacred cultures. How often, for example, has the desire for union with God expressed itself in sexual metaphors, whether in the *Book of Solomon*, the poems of Donne, the ecstasies of the mystics—whether Sufis or saints? Why has orgasm been called *le petit morte* unless it is experienced as assuagement of painful, estranging consciousness—founded as it is on an obligatory separation from the other—through an ecstatic fusion with the other? Why is birthing a baby or producing a work of art painful yet joyous, if we are not in service to an archetypal energy that transcends even our desire for comfort and security?

Our common existential condition is separation. We are traumatically separated from the Other at birth, live a life of estrangement from others, yet perpetually desire reconnection, homecoming. The psychological health of the child often depends on how and to what degree this separation trauma is mediated by supportive, affirming parents. And our subsequent maturity as adults similarly depends on the degree to which one can tolerate one's separation from others and cultivate a relationship to one's self. As one person who was reluctant to end a bad relationship said to me, "I won't let go of this hand in the darkness until another hand is there." And another person, having lost her husband through a sudden heart attack, in her first hour of therapy asked, "Who will walk with me to the bathroom in the middle of the night?" When I gently replied that *she* would prove to be the one who would accompany herself to the bathroom, she got up and walked out of therapy forever. These are moments when Eros prevails without the counterbalancing of Logos, the necessary energy of separation, development, and differentiation.

◆　◆　◆

When we begin to look at the role of Eros in the lives of women and men we find that no formulary satisfactorily embraces us all. We are all different, unique, and we contradict and confound generalizations; yet there are patterns that we have generated over time with which we characteristically associate women and men.* For both, Eros is about connection, albeit in differing forms and stratagems.

The old, old debates between nature and nurture, between genetics and cultural context, persist because the matter is complex, and because both force fields play a role. Sexual identity and sexual preference are biologically driven, yet are greatly influenced by social construct as well. When we consider, for example, how so many get bent out of shape by homosexuality, we need to remind them that it has always existed, both in humans and other animals, that the percentage of gay persons is roughly constant around the world, suggesting a genetic determinant, and thereby not a

---

* I am well aware that the mere discussion of these issues is controversial, complex, and that contradictory evidence may be found for every assertion made; however, I do think that our reflecting together here may yet prove provocative and productive for self-awareness.

"lifestyle choice." The misguided theological efforts to change homosexual preference is better spent on changing one's own ignorance of scientific, cultural, and social facts, and, even more, of curbing one's anxieties about one's own sexual grounding, as well as profuse other ambiguities that are unsettling to personal comfort. Moreover, is it not a closeted blasphemy to challenge the same "deity" who created our genders and sexual identities and preferences in the first place?

Across the spectrum of Eros's ministries, there are infinite varieties of expression, although the social constructs through which they are perceived are rather clumsily defined and delimited. When we consider how Eros shows up in women's lives we find that it is *most* commonly expressed through relationship; that is, for most women, most energy is invested and most satisfaction is found in the quality of relatedness to others, be they partner, child, or friend. For most men, Eros expresses itself predominantly in goal-directed behaviors. Obviously, both genders have many manifestations of the other as well, as women focus their efforts on their goals, and men profit from affective interaction with others. As the Spanish Jungian analyst Irene de Castillejo once differentiated, one has more commonly embodied the life force through "diffuse awareness" and the other through "focused awareness." Which one is right? Both obviously are necessary, although shifting cultural contexts will sometimes favor one over the other. Either way, the reliance on one, and the neglect of the other, will, for both genders, ultimately exact a substantial price.

For men, narrowly focused on their external task, a progressive estrangement from their inner life often results.

They look for satisfaction in their external attainments, be it panting after what William James called "the bitch goddess Success," or public acclaim, or money, or a sense of achievement, and typically expect their partner to provide them emotional nurturance as equilibrium. They are partially driven by their nature, partly by the messages of their tribe to separate from their ground, whether it be home, or mother, and partially driven by their cultural imperatives to find their value in the external world.

This estrangement from instinct and from relatedness to others leads to a profound loneliness. As I have written elsewhere, the best way for women to understand the life of the typical man would be to imagine that they: 1) remove from themselves their closest friends, those with whom they share their deepest secrets, fears, hopes; 2) sever linkage to an internal guidance system, whether they call it their instincts, intuition, or feeling life; and 3) measure their worth predominantly through their capacity to attain external, abstract standards of productivity. (This portrait of a psychological wasteland appalls most women, but then at least they understand men's lives better. Women who compete in this patriarchal construct soon suffer the same miseries as men, albeit with an enhanced capacity and permission to diagnose themselves and buy out of the script.)

While women's lives have historically been disempowered and miserable, for which men are in large measure responsible, men's lives, because of the price of self-estrangement, are perhaps even more miserable and pathetic. They are the endangered gender. Because of this self-estrangement, men, generally denied access to "the feminine" within them, and derided for efforts to connect to "her," have conveyed too much psychological power to women and then wind up either trying to control her, or please her, or avoid her. For this reason, though driven biologically, sexuality occupies too large a role, psychologically speaking, in the psychic economy of men. The fastest-growing addiction in our time is the Internet, and the largest number of Web pages and Web hits are to pornographic sites. These sites offer superficial, but seemingly noncostly access to the "feminine," just as drugs and alcohol have offered for millennia. Sadly, it not only objectifies women, creates impossible standards and expectations for men and the real women in their lives, but only deepens the split men carry from what Jung called their *anima*.

The *anima*, a Latin word for *soul*, is a metaphor for man's inner life, his relationship to the body, to instinct, to feeling, to values, to spiritual aspiration. Split off from his own anima, a man will suffer depression, anger, homelessness, and a proclivity to seek "her" in the outer world. The more he looks outside himself, the more he will suffer her absence. He thinks he will find her through a woman, or some sublimated surrogate, but these connections, powerful and rich as they may be, can only partially treat the great wound to the soul's agenda within. Hence, his experience of Eros is typically to project his anima upon success, a woman, or an abstract value, but end by being dispirited, angry, and depressed. We can see, therefore, that the average man, now and through history, will be looking for something profound, something seductive, something compelling, "out there," and he will grow further and further from finding that he has lost contact with her "in here."

Typically, men's Eros projections of the anima show up

in 1) the figure of Eve, that is, instinctual sexuality; 2) the Mother, source of nurturance; 3) the muse, or the inspiring woman, as Beatricca was to Dante; or 4) the source of nature's wisdom, Sophia. So much literature and fine art, so many cultural pursuits, so many projections, so much energy have been generated from these intrapsychic imagoes—yet the anima grows more and more remote from the lives of most men. Yet may we not remember the condign advice of poet Friedrich Hölderlin, that "that which thou seekest is near, and already coming to meet thee."

For the woman, Jung's term *animus** represents her sense of "empowerment," namely, her sense of personal worth, psychological *gravitas*, permission for and capacity to *do* her life *in* the world. If the *anima* for men represents the life-sustaining soul, the *animus* for women represents her spirited energy for achieving life on her own terms. When the woman's inner animus is supportive, "he" legitimizes her desires and helps her achieve them. When the animus is negative, "he" undermines her confidence, impugns her worth, and divides her energy in doubt, desuetude, deflection of eros, and depression. When the animus is not consciously present for her, women will project them outward, as men do the anima. The popular-culture forms of these projections are 1) the Tarzan, or man of brute strength; 2) the hero, or doer of deeds; 3) the man of logos, word, intellect, or the power of expression; and 4) the sage, or man of transcendent, spiritual wisdom. Claiming each of those roles, capacities, and tasks for herself proves critical to her maturational development.

---

* The masculine ending of the Latin for "soul," which he translated as "spirit."

Naturally, and appropriately, these stereotypes are criticized today for their culture-bound gender limitations, but we still see multitudinous expressions of these projections in our movies, songs, sitcoms, and customs. (For example, if a songwriter wrote a sequential lyric about the search for the beloved Other, the meeting with that wonderful Other, the noisy traffic with that Other, the conflicts with that fractious Other, the loss of that Other, and the renewed search for that Other, he or she would catch everyone at some stage of their history with the Other, and thereby write the all-time love song, especially if it is a country-and-western song and a long-eared dog is thrown in the mix.) Though easily parodied, such culture forms would not occupy such a ubiquitous part of our popular culture if they did not speak to something profound within our unconscious lives. We are not drawn to, or moved by, something that does not touch a place deep within us.

Where a conscious relationship to Eros is not present, where men or women do not have modeling, permission, or affirmation to connect to this telluric energy, then they will suffer splits from their own guiding instincts, feel disconnected from the transcendent, and engage in futile, but compulsive, searches for what is missing inwardly in the outer world. Who among us has not in fact sought the source of nurturance and empowerment—our mutual, twin needs—in the beloved Other? Who has not been shaped by, perhaps wounded by, cultural expressions of this search? Who is immune to the seductions of fantasy, and thereby neglected the fact, or never knew, that the godly powers reside within us from the beginning? When Jung once said that "a neurosis is an offended god," he meant, metaphorically, that the neglect of a deep, instinctual energy ultimately revenges itself in our somatic discords, compulsions, addictions, or projections onto others. Count on the fact that *whatever we deny within, we will compulsively seek in the outer world instead.* When we have not valued *Eros as the search for greater knowledge of self and world*, then we are far more likely to become enslaved to our projects and projections—whether sex, substance, symbol, or relational addiction—for nothing holds greater power over us than our unconsciousness, which perforce makes decisions on our behalf throughout the conduct of daily life.

◆ ◆ ◆

Generally speaking, women have a better, more nuanced relationship to Eros than men, for they are psychologically more likely to find the ministries of the god in varied venues. Men, having so often equated the god with success in their endeavors, are devastated by retirement, impotence of any kind, defeat, or displacement. Sadly, they are more likely to drift into sadness, depression, substance abuse, suicide, compulsive sexuality, or seek some quick surrogate lover or diverting cause. Accordingly, they handle the death of a marriage or spouse, retirement, or occupational displacement poorly because they have lost contact with their inner soul life. Women also suffer these losses deeply but usually have a more differentiated relationship to Eros, having developed over time a network of supportive friends, hobbies, varied activities, abundant sources of conversation, and typically a more evolved relationship to their guiding, intuitive centers.

It has been said that the best treatment plan for loneliness is solitude. In solitude one is not alone; one is present to oneself, from whence a goodly conversation may emerge. If, in general, most women have developed a relationship to their inner life, then they, in addition to their supportive network, may effectively treat loneliness with solitude. This engagement of Eros through relationship to one's instinctual self works better for women than the typical stratagems of men, who seek a new relation to the outer anima, anesthetize their pain, or sink into depression. Each seeks transcendence of the existential trials of life through the god Eros, but their strategies and results vary greatly. While men have generally suffered their estrangement unconsciously, women have more commonly learned that honoring the god Eros requires taking care of themselves, maintaining their health and relationships, and staying in touch with the guiding instincts that more adequately lead us through the world, and, over time, bring us more nearly home to ourselves. Women are more likely to grieve necessary losses openly, and therefore with a measure of psychological honesty, while men usually attempt to bury or deflect. But, as we know, what is pushed under invariably surfaces somewhere else.

◆ ◆ ◆

I recently spoke with a very thoughtful, retired man who has handled retirement better than anyone I know, having gone back to pick up the spiritual pieces of the puzzle left behind while spending his earlier life making money. Nonetheless, he spoke of how an early, archaic, persistent desire for approval still periodically captivated him and obliged demonstrating his insight and guiding wisdom to corporate boards on which he still served. While acknowledging need for the approval of others, critical to the self-worth of a child, and still a normal desire of a normal adult, he knows that this urgency represents a piece of his unfinished business. Having spent his life in the business of making money and wielding power, he clearly understands what "business" is required of him today. Learning to value the dialogue he has been establishing with his inner life, and the many unmet aspects of the soul, is how the business of healing is presently occurring and will continue to occur for him. After making a specific personal inventory, his soul has eagerly responded to his immersion in Eastern spirituality, travel to places of historic significance, in-depth studies of psychology and philosophy, rodeo photography—all enthusiasms left behind in the youthful summons to serve the great god Economics. While retired, Eros drives him still, but in service to values long crowded out by external pressures and provisional roles, values nonetheless long requested by the soul.

◆ ◆ ◆

Remember that to speak of Eros as a *god* is not to make a theological or metaphysical assertion; it is rather to metaphorically underline its archetypal, universal, profound power in our lives. If we think of "the gods" as embodied energies, then we have not only a means of making such energies available to consciousness, but we offer our respect to the autonomy, transcendence, and omnipresence of those powers in our lives. The devolution of the all-powerful Eros into the little dude with diapers and bow and arrow, Cupid, is a diminution of respect. Cupid may be powerful, but he is expressive only of infant possibilities, and occasions no lasting respect for the archaic, energic fundament upon which all life is based. That Cupid has become a cultural icon for romance and valentines, just as the Devil has become a sports mascot, is suggestive of how these powerful images devolve from symbols, which once pointed beyond themselves toward the mystery, to signs, which, as mere concepts, are encapsulated in the ego's limitations and ultimately trivialized.

Recently I was speaking with a man who has lost all erotic attraction to his wife, an event puzzling to him and sorrowful to her. His Eros is of course not gone, because the gods never go away; but they may go elsewhere.* So where is the god Eros for him? Is it invested in work, in another, in some projected value, or is it withdrawn by illness or the psyche into the unconscious? This man is sad, but not depressed. He is busy, but not obsessed by his work. He suffers no discernible illness, but he has lost contact with the god. As I write, we are trying to track this incognito deity and trace where he is gone.

In praising the power of Eros, Freud did us all a favor, but he also contributed to its being too narrowly defined in sexual venues. Yes, he did articulate the powerful idea of *sublimation*, whereby the "sexual" instinct, when blocked from its primary object, may differentiate and distribute into substitutionary gratification, such as work, art, and "higher" cultural forms. Jung also recognized the power of Eros, but rather he thought of its many cultural forms not as secondary elaborations of a primary agenda, but as intrinsic to our holistic search for meaning. We are, he asserted,

---

* We will deal with this issue in a later chapter when we consider why *the gods* are *verbs*, not nouns, and where they are today.

symbol-making, symbol creating animals. When, for example, the average life span was thirty at best, why would one spend one's short life building a cathedral whose construction might take four centuries, knowing that one would never see the finished wonder? Or, for that matter, why would a parent be willing to sacrifice for its child, knowing that the child is also death-bound, and likely to follow a path quite different from the parent's expectations? Is it not a bit too much to ascribe this to sexuality, even sexuality differentiated? Would it not be better to reverse this identification and say that sexuality is but one expression, in one venue, varied as it is, of this life force, this elemental energy that is seeking to become in the world through all its forms in service to ends that remain profoundly mysterious to us? Is not Eros as a god mysterious and beyond our understanding, after all? Is not Eros found in all forms of human expression?

Let us remember that what the gods ask of us is that we remember them, respect them. When we remember the power of Eros, we serve life itself; we serve the mysterious ends that move us, moved our predecessors, and will move our descendants. When we lose contact with Eros we have lost contact with life. Occasionally, all of us lose this contact. We are distracted, fatigued, satiated, and depressed. We are forgetful of our summons to the gods, and rather give over to our unforgiving, narrowing neuroses. Someone recently said to me, "I have nothing left to do. I should go now," meaning "die." I replied that while many tasks were done in her life, Eros always summons us anew, and up to our last breath we are in service to its numinous summons.

As a therapist, one always has to ask where the life is, where Eros moves, what it asks of us, in even our most wretched conditions. Paradoxically, one often finds that the painfully presented symptoms we wish to remove or repress are themselves the expression of Eros, perhaps wounded Eros. Healing our souls requires tracking the movement of Eros in our projections onto others, or perhaps tracing the faded footsteps of Eros to the bottom of our depressions, where Eros awaits reunion with us. Following the tale-telling bread crumbs through our emotional forests—or, to switch allusions, Ariadne's thread through the labyrinth we all carry within—is the task of consciousness, the task of therapy, the task of recovering right relationship to the gods.

Let me give some examples. When we address why a depression has fallen upon us, or why we suffer panic attacks, or why we repeatedly sabotage ourselves, we have to track the "logic" of our symptom down to what the soul wants from us. (Our symptoms are "logical" expressions of an inner conflict, an embodiment of the contretemps between oppression and expression.) Why, in a depression, has "the committee of the inner life" withdrawn cooperation from the agenda of the CEO ego? What do "they" want? Why has generalized anxiety, which is an inescapable aspect of our existential condition, chosen this venue for its panicky focus? What task must be faced by consciousness to free up our Eros to its preferred ends, even while swimming in anxiety? How are we still subject to an old, archaic message about our worth, manifesting as a noisome tendency for repetitive self-sabotage? From whence comes that insistent message, given us by whom, and what counter-behavior is required as compensation?

In these investigations of wounded Eros, and the symptoms that undermine consciousness as problems, we are invited to clear the underbrush away for a fuller natural expression of life. This self-examination does not lead to our being "well adjusted," nor will it likely win the plaudits of others, but it does lead to a greater authenticity. Theologian Paul Tillich once defined sin as "inauthentic being," and Jung defined neurosis as the choice of inauthentic suffering over authentic suffering. Apparently, in the latter, the gods rather than the neuroses are served.

In my view, the first great work of depth psychology in the modern era, and paean to Eros before Freud, is Dostoyevsky's *Notes From Underground*. In this 1863 work, Dostoyevsky depicts in embarrassing detail the narcissistic, shadowy agendas that course beneath the world of civilization and disrupt or contradict its professed values. While a scorching critique of our self-delusory tendencies, in the end Dostoyevsky nonetheless praises our irrational energies, our desire-driven circus of Eros whereby we demonstrate that we are human, and not merely piano keys to be struck and to resonate in programmed, predictable ways.* His prophetic horror was that we lose touch with even the perverse permutations of Eros, becoming the programmed person so many of the systems of the next century did produce, systems that created anonymity, depersonalization, robotic responses, and conditioned values.

The portrait of humanity Dostoyevsky depicts is troubling and apparently contradictory to our ego ideals, but as Jung noted, a shadowless person proves to be a superficial

---

* Too much of modern psychology demeans the richness and complexity of the human by limiting its scope of inquiry and treatment to operant conditioning, or cognitive and behavioral process. We are the creatures who demand meaning, suffer its absence, and twist ourselves in painfully tropic ways to find its light.

person. The Underground Man is spiteful, jealous, selfish, and hurtful to his beloved. In other words, he is like us. Still, the Underground Man is also willing to acknowledge his pettiness, his narcissism in ways we camouflage, even from ourselves. Distasteful as he is, he *is* us, and his life is a vivid expression of Eros in all its multiform possibilities. His is not a pretty portrait, but it is one that most fully offers a diapason to the disparate claims of the diverse divinities driving our humanity.

In the journey each of us lives, Eros is the guide of the quickened soul. Most of us learned early to distrust our desire, shy away from the large task that stands before us. Generally we seek comfort over enlargement, reassurance over risk, and seldom venture out beyond the predictable. Our dilemma is not that we are capable of both so much evil and so much self-denial, but that we are capable of so much spiritual pettiness. It may prove a "terrible" thing to be summoned before the large, before the call of the numinous, but it is in those moments that we express our journey most fully.

The gods never go away. They go underground and reappear somewhere else. Figuring out where they have gone, how they, like Proteus, have reincarnated in another form, is our first move toward healing. The ego has little control over this encounter, for where the gods wish to take us—to profound love, or madness, or desire—is beyond our limited powers. While we remain responsible for our choices and their consequences, the ego is invited to respect those powers, the denial of which will sooner or later produce consequences that we could scarcely have imagined.

All gods demand respect, whether we like them or fear them. Standing in a more conscious relationship to Eros is standing in right relationship to life itself. Wounded Eros seeks to heal; but neglected Eros seeks revenge, and will sooner or later create monsters. The Swiss ambassador to Berlin once quoted Hitler at a 1930s reception: "I should have been an architect, but now it is too late." What diseased permutations this Austrian corporal's wounded Eros, disfigured and neglected, brought into this world, and how healing a life creating art might have otherwise been for him, and for this troubled world. Either way Eros will emerge—whether in constructing or burning buildings. Jung, quoting Erasmus, carved over the entrance to his home in Küsnacht, Switzerland, CALLED OR NOT CALLED, GOD WILL BE THERE.* Called or not called, Eros nonetheless calls us. Tracking such a god will always lead us further into the rich jungle of life.

To serve that god, we are called to know ourselves (every crevice we can manage, or bear), called to acknowledge even that which seems unlovable within us, and called to explore every facet of the soul's unfolding mystery that surges beneath the flux of our daily life. As poet Paul Celan discovered, "Reality is not simply there, it must be searched and won." To stir with desire is to serve life, no matter how wounded, dispossessed, and alone we feel. Even today, Tennyson's Victorian portrait of the aging Ulysses, scarred by combat, haunted by the ghosts of his many losses, longing again for the perils of the wine-dark sea, remains a fitting portrait of our essential condition. Eros calls, love summons, and quite probably new disasters beckon as well:

---

* That phrase in Latin, *Vocatus et non Vocatus Deus Aderit*, borrowed from Erasmus, is also respectfully carved over the entrance to the Jung Center of Houston, TX.

Old age hath yet his honor and his toil.
Death closes all; but something ere the end,
Some work of noble note, may yet be done,
Not unbecoming men that strove with gods.
. . . . Come, my friends,
*'Tis not too late to seek a newer world.**

Yes, it is clear, disasters of one kind or another will finally overthrow our constructed worlds, but the journey is interesting, you have to admit. And so, called or not, this protean god Eros presides over all, and perversely calls us into life through the permutations of desire. We may forget Eros, but whether to trial, tragedy, or triumph, Eros does not forget us.

◆ ◆ ◆

Do you recall Angela in the first paragraph of this chapter? In our last analytic hour she said, "I sacrificed my marriage to love. I knew I did not love my husband, and he deserved someone who did. And I deserved someone whom I could love. My mother screamed at me for this decision, that it was against our religion." We know, however, that Angela enacted a difficult but religious sacrifice to a god whose name is Eros.

---

* Tennyson, "Ulysses," ll. 50ff.

Chapter Five

THAT WE STEP INTO LARGENESS

*J*ung's homey proverb that most of the time, "we walk in shoes too small for us," reminds us that the necessity of adaptation to the voices around us, the demands of our environment, require that we mostly live through adaptive psychologies rather than being guided by an instinctually driven center that wishes embodiment through us into the world. Additionally, his metaphor suggests that on most days we suffer a failure of nerve. Living "small" is easier than living large. Living "large" is not narcissistic inflation,* but rather encountered in the daily summons to risk being who we are.

Recently I worked with a man who is seventy and retiring from his profession. What beckoned him—promising peace, stepping down from the pressures, offering freedom to pursue his interests—has proved to be rather problematic after all. It seems that in the decades of faithfully serving the expectations of his family, his church, his profession, he has essentially lost contact with his own needs, his own instinctual reality. Like so many people I meet, he does not feel an essential permission to be who he is, desire what he wants,

---

* As American "philosopher" Pearl Bailey once said, "Thems what thinks they is, ain't."

and pursue what the soul wants. How incredible is this fact that a person can live a productive life, be approved of by family and culture, and have achieved every conscious goal, and still have no "permission."

Is not this issue pretty general among us? When we are young we are fully persuaded that we are in charge of our lives, and plunging toward our appointed destiny. We cannot afford to have too many doubts; therefore, forward always! Concomitantly, we grow identified with our roles—as partner, parent, and provider. Later, we may question why, if we have served those roles faithfully, they may not have reciprocally served us. Later, we may gain enough strength, or feel desperate enough, to question, to look back and to ask, "Just who am I apart from those roles?" "Who am I apart from my history and my assigned script?" Or we may ask, "*Why* am I here, really?" Then we are often disconcerted to realize that we do not know the answer to those deepest questions. Frequently, we do not know who we are, what we are doing, or in service to what. Only rarely do we realize that somewhere along the way we lost psychological "permission" to be who we really are.

The issue of "permission" tracks back to an elemental fact of our journey's origin. Our experience of the world *is* conditional. We are subject to the conditions fate presents to us—our genetics, our family of origins and its core dynamics, and our zeitgeist. All of these social settings embody messages, and demand a measure of compliance. The one message all of us received is this: "The world is big, and you are not. The world is powerful, and you are not. Now, spend the next few decades coping with that fact, buster."

We are necessarily obliged to adapt, even as we absorb

those messages as "ours," as the apparently irrefutable nature of the world, as the fundamental construct and conditions of reality. These necessary internalizations of messages, these adaptations to their demands, these scripts, mean that we progressively lose contact with our own instinctual guidance. Thus, for most of us, the issue of "permission" to be who we are—separate, distinct, individual sojourners with differing goals—remains denied within. No matter how much we have attained in the world, we are often stunned to realize that we may have lost contact totally with who we are, that is, whomever the gods intended.

We find, perhaps to our dismay, that we are instead *who* or *what* we became in our adaptations. Recently, a well-known teen idol sheared her hair in public. Over and over, in radio interviews for a previous book, I was asked how a person could do such a "crazy" thing, when she was obviously living a privileged life, a life much coveted by many others. (Why so many intelligent people would even be interested in *any-thing* she did is another question.) So, let us ask what the psyche is saying in this "craziness."

Surely she is testifying to the horror of being the "project" of so many projections, which celebrity demands.* Surely she is unwittingly "confessing" to herself and to the world that some resistant part of her realizes that she is not who she is construed by others to be, that she is so encapsulated by celebrity that she now lacks vital linkage to herself. Perhaps this early meltdown, this early recognition of inter-

---

* When, in *No Exit*, Jean-Paul Sartre exclaims that "Hell is other people," he elsewhere explains that one's humanity is often constricted and delimited by being "the project" of other people's projections. T. S. Eliot's "Prufrock" similarly complains of being fixated by other people's opinions like an insect upon a wall.

nal discrepancy will provide her with the ample space and time to walk away from stardom and reclaim the girl she was, and become the woman she can be. It is much more likely that the seduction of "success," and the self-interest of an entourage who suck off of her, will pull her back into an identification with her celebrity. What Jung called "the regressive restoration of the persona" will likely oblige her psyche to pathologize in ever more compelling rebellions. Her dilemma is simply a caricature of the dilemma we all have encountered, an identification with our adaptations, a confusion of the Self with our persona. Sooner or later, a great distress will rise from our soul to trouble us, perplex us, dismay us, but which, if we can possibly query it to find what it wants from us, will prove to be our best friend.

While so many have laughed at her act, ridiculed her, or sought some pathological category in which to place her,* it may well be that her psyche has mobilized to save her from her glass-bubble existence. Ask yourself, why might *you* voluntarily cut off your hair, and in public no less? And ask yourself, what might it mean if you did? Is it to garner more publicity? She already has too much. Is it a sign of "mental breakdown"? Or is such self-destructive behavior her psyche's way of buying out of the Devil's bargain?

Many teenage girls would trade their lives in a heartbeat for the life of a celebrity. They wish, after all, to be seen, to feel special, to be valued by others. They wish to be the cynosure of the attentiveness of others, even though they

---

* By judgmental pathologizing, one may thereby distance oneself from a recognition of one's own madness. As Dostoyevsky once observed in *A Writer's Diary*, "Is it not by locking up one's neighbor that one convinces oneself of one's own good sense."

already resent the hovering scrutiny of their parents and their teachers. How would they then feel, after the original rush of excitement, the high of adulation, to be watched constantly, especially by those looking for any screw-up? How would they then feel if they knew that they were locked in that role, and guaranteed no surcease, privacy, or ability to change their minds? They would grow to hate their roles, their celebrity, although they might be loathe to let go of its perks. Then their psyches would have to take over where consciousness faltered. They would suffer anxiety attacks, depressions; they would medicate their dis-ease with booze and pills; they would escalate the razzmatazz values of their plastic world further to get some ever larger buzz. And so the psyche will have to counter-escalate in return. Just think of the obvious examples—Marilyn, Elvis, Anna Nicole, and hosts of others—to see the burnout, the self-destruction, the breakdowns of the false self. Psyche knows, and will not forever tolerate our abuse of it.

Underneath this child's symbolic act is a profound desire for an authentic life. To shear her womanly pride, her hair, to shed her corona, is to say to all of us that she can no longer bear this constrictive definition of her soul, no longer prop up this constructed self, and must radically deconstruct it in order to break free. Still, the day I write these sentences she has checked herself in and out of the second, perhaps third, rehab, having stayed in each for less than one day.

She is understandably clinging to the false self, as we all have, and do, seduced still by its glitter; so, psyche must now surely escalate further, and meet her again in some other garden. One is reminded of the Iranian parable of the man who meets Death while working in his master's vineyard. He asks his master for the loan of a fast horse to flee to Samara. The wish is granted. Later, while walking the fields, the master happens upon Death and expresses his dismay that His Spectral Eminence had frightened his servant. To this, Death replies, "I did not mean to frighten him. I only expressed my astonishment at finding him still here when we have an appointment later tonight in Samara." So, psyche waits for us, and meets us somewhere else. Even if we try to forget that appointment, psyche will not.

◆ ◆ ◆

Still another way in which we refuse to step into largeness is by way of holding on to the past, especially the limiting past. We hold on to grudges, slights, injuries, past wounding and allow them to dominate our present. I once saw a woman for one hour, if that long. She came to complain that her two married, adult sons never came around, never honored her holidays or her anniversaries. She vehemently denigrated them and her former husband—their father—blamed their wives for this turn of events, and in general whined about her life. It was not hard to see why they would not want to visit. When, delicately, I suggested as much to her, that she might consider acting in a more accepting, less punitive way with them, she launched into an attack on me as well. Then she got up and left . . . to my relief.

Similarly, when we find people grinding away decades after their bitter divorce, or when they are continuously complaining that no one is taking care of them, then we realize that such a person has not stepped into a larger life. They have, consciously or unconsciously, presumed that someone was going to take care of them, make sense of life for them, rescue them from the ambiguities and sufferings of ordinary life, and, in general, shield them from having to grow up. How many move back into their adult children's neighborhood—in the name of parental devotion, of course—but covertly expect the child to take care of their emotional needs now? Because they have not accepted the challenge of their own life, they refuse to grow up, refuse to step into larger shoes. They will likely die this way, unloved and unloving, because their outraged narcissism refuses to look inward and accept responsibility for what they find there. As children, we have a right to look to others to take care of us, protect us, nurture us, show us the way. Sometimes we get that; sometimes we do not. Either way, we all have to grow up, become wholly responsible for our lives, relinquish the search for the good parent in others, and stop whining.

Members of a civic organization I know once lived in mutual dependency and self-congratulatory fusion. When their organization took steps to modernize, they berated the board for no longer providing "community." But their community was the collusion of the dependent, and few if any grew, were empowered, or enlarged beyond their neediness. This was quite satisfactory to them for decades. It was much easier to blame others, to host pity parties, and to stay stuck. No one—the person, their partners, their children, their society—were served by this dependency, this neediness, or this refusal to grow up.

Still, we must admit that there is a part of each of us that is needy, frightened, intimidated, and dependent. Thinking that such an archaic, and therefore autonomous, part is not there and waiting to enlist others in its demands, is simply naive and unconscious. Trying to not let that part dominate our life is a perpetual challenge, but it remains our chief contribution to others to lift this task off of them and take it on for ourselves.

This neediness sabotages our relationships, shows up in simplistic theologies and politics, and infantilizes our culture. I live near two of the American mega-churches, and weekly I see the thousands trudging into sanctuaries to hear their guru speak. I wonder if any that day will have an enlarging experience. I wonder if any will be called to grow in the face of their fears—make that our common fears—or reclaim personal authority, spiritual maturity, when it might result in estrangement and loneliness. I wonder if any will be summoned to a truly larger life, or will they consign themselves to someone else telling them what to think, how to live, and what to value. When their presumptive contract with life betrays them, which is to say, asks something really large from them, will they then blame "God," or castigate themselves for the weakness of their applied will? Too often the fundamentalist factions of our culture either terrify people into compliance—and I will never forgive them for that spiritual violence—or seduce people into the ratification of their complexes by validating the easy materialism and narcissism in which we all swim.

A culture driven by the trivial has seldom matured sufficiently to look at itself. How can we expect to find and elect leaders who will in fact provide vision, summon us to the realistic costs of growth and interaction in the world community, and effectively deal with the reality that all important issues have nuances and ambiguities? Why do we not have leadership that says to us, respectfully and candidly, that the problems we face, at home and abroad, are complex, that no choice is without its costs, and that patience, humility, dialogue, and a larger grasp of complexity will be required of all of us? Are we so immature that we need someone to protect us from ourselves, to lie to us, to collude with our lack of intellectual discipline, our difficulty in handling complexity, our immaturity? Why do we not have more theologians, or preachers, who confirm that life involves suffering, and that our deepest questions will never fully be answered? Why do we have psychologists in the media who conveniently fail to verify the contradictions with which we all daily live, the necessary suffering that is a by-product of real life, rather than suggest that three easy steps will bring us happiness and material affluence? Until we grow up and step into the large challenge of living our journey as individuals and as a society, we will get the demagogic leaders and the infantilizing culture we deserve. These external artifacts reflect what we have not addressed within.

◆　◆　◆

All of us have to ask this simple but piercing question of our relationships, our affiliations, our professions, our politics, and our theology: "Does this path, this choice, make me larger or smaller?" Usually we know the answer immediately because we always intuitively know, and yet are afraid of what we know, and even more afraid of what it may ask of us. If we do not sincerely know, then we need to continue asking the question until it reveals itself to us, as it inevitably will. Then the real task begins. (Jung once said that every therapist should ask the question, "What task is this person's neurosis helping him or her avoid?") We recognize in those moments of revelation what life is asking us to do, where we need to grow up. And what then are we going to do about it? Are we going to deny, repress, blame others, shuffle about a bit, dance some dilatory doo-dah until we die, or finally grow up, step into largeness, become an adult?

Allied with this intimidation by the large is a phenomenon I have seen that, at the outset, seems improbable. Time and time again I encounter people who have achieved notable work—raised their families, supported themselves, contributed to the world—yet who do not inwardly feel legitimate, or consider themselves in the ranks of "real" persons who are entitled to truly feel what they feel, desire what they desire, pursue what summons them. While all of us are creatures of adaptation, these folks in particular early on "read" their environment for messages about who they are, what they are to do and not do, and what they are to value. Our provisional selves, our counterfeit identities, are essentially anxiety-management systems. These systems have so much power, so much autonomy, are so deeply buried in our psyches that we seldom know their presence, understand the delegated authority they carry, and the extent to which they govern our lives. Only when we pay attention to our symptoms, our patterns, our painful encounters with ourselves may we begin to discern these alien, implanted "ideas" to which our history has so long been in service. Only when we look at the patterns of our personal history do we see the autonomy granted to those invisible systems, complexes, that create the recurrent motifs, outcomes, and hierarchies of values that constitute our outer, visible histories.

Daily I sit with individuals, usually in their fifties or sixties, who have acquired enough emotional maturity, enough history upon which to reflect, and enough ego strength to bear unpleasant truths. One man discovered that his life of outer, driven accomplishment had been, covertly, to prove to his mother that *her* life was worth something. A woman who suffered profound emotional neglect lived a life of self-sabotage because she, having never been mirrored by her parents, could never see the good soul she was. When she looked in her own mirror, no one stared back. Accordingly, her life partners all proved narcissists, whom she chose, precisely, albeit unconsciously, because they would reconfirm this archaic portrait of herself. Another woman was chronically depressed. Fate had chosen to bring a sibling with cerebral palsy into her family. Watching her little brother with such a catastrophic handicap, such legitimate need, watching her parents understandably devoting their lives to his care, she acquired the message that she was not entitled to ask anything for herself. This was not an inaccurate reading of the family dynamics, but as a plan for her subsequent, adult life, it proved reductive, repetitive, and depression-generating.

Additionally, a significant percentage of my practice over the last twenty years has been with other therapists as clients,* and with therapist groups as a speaker, from which, inevitably, the theme of "the wounded healer" emerges. The preponderant number of people in the care-giving professions—nurses,

---

* As one psychologist said to me in our first hour, "We all know that when it comes time to do our own work, we go to a psychodynamic therapist." He was a trained behaviorist who also partnered with a psychiatrist, and both were into a great deal of pharmacology. I always wondered what would happen if the public knew what professional therapists know, that the real work of growth and healing is time consuming, and requires a depth of exploration not provided by most therapeutic modalities, not to mention the "managed care" fantasy contrived to benefit insurance companies.

social workers, clergy, therapists—come from troubled families of origin. As children they learned to subordinate their needs, to hone, bevel, truncate their spontaneous personalities in service to stabilizing their family dynamics, or to be enlisted as scapegoats for unresolved adult issues, and all ardently sought to heal their parents in whatever way possible. This impossible but compelling task is so deeply imprinted in their lives that as adults they remain identified with this role. While many *can* do very good work because of their insights and empathy, almost all continue to suffer intrapsychic turbulence as their own troubled family dynamics are re-created through their clients.

Their family of origin could not be healed, for that was beyond the powers of the child; and now the world cannot be healed, for another and another wounded soul is lined up just after the one they just treated. Thus, symbiotically, they are wed to this endless task, and are hourly subjected to stress that activates their own archaic field of anxieties, depressions, and yet compulsive commitments. When they seek to leave this agitated environment, this task, they are afflicted with crippling "guilt." Their guilt is not real guilt, for they are doing nothing wrong when they seek to take care of themselves, to save the only person they can save; it is rather an anxiety that is activated by stepping out from under their archaic assignment. (My rough guess is that perhaps 50 percent of professional caregivers should be in the field, and 50 percent should not. This latter group will inevitably bring harm to *someone*—if not the client, parishioner, patient, then themselves—when their own archaic wounds are activated, as they are daily. And from outside, one cannot tell to which half each person belongs.)

This special category of professional caregivers who typically do not have permission to have their own lives, with an agenda driven by the soul rather than the adaptations obliged by fate, is definitive and identifiable. But it is generally true that most of us have neither permission nor feelings of authenticity. Coming from a working-class family, where work was synonymous with survival, worth, and integrity, I have always found it difficult not to work. This family ethic was reinforced by early religious training that emphasized the primacy of "good works" as a spiritual path. Even on vacation I find it difficult, as Walt Whitman put it, to invite the soul to loaf. I have always needed to be doing something to keep the wolf from the door, or to be doing something constructive or contributive to the world. Being "lazy" was the worst thing I could imagine. The legacy of our Puritan past, with its implicit equation of work with the blessings of divinity, are enmeshed with the idea of productivity as a gender value and as a measure of psychological worth. The problem with this formula, however, is that the judgment of "lazy" is prejudicial and reductive. Doing what the soul wants rather than what the complexes want is not being lazy. It is serving a larger agenda than our archaic biographies permit. So, pun intended, I am still "working" on this issue. At least I know where I need to work.

As we get to this point in our life we see that stepping into a larger life is intimidating because it requires that we risk being who we really are, that is, what wants to come to the world through us, rather than serving our ego comforts or whatever instructions came our way. We cannot expect someone else to give us permission. The parent complexes, or the culture complexes, are embedded in history, and never will stop saying what they always said. (They possess a stunted imagination.) So, it is up to us at this later point, when we have served those voices so long, to realize that our own psyches have a unique point of view, that each of us is different, and are bound for different destinies. Even siblings are bound for separate journeys, and all of us, at the end of our life, will have to answer as to what we did with our summons.

Stepping into largeness will require that we discern our personal authority—rather than the authority of others or the authority of our internalized admonitions—and live this inner authority with risk and boldness. A colleague has been leading a women's group in her church and over and over she has heard, "And what is it we believe on this matter?" Is it not sad that people of a certain age have not thought for themselves on issues of such importance to them and need to ask, "What is it we believe?" Do they ask advertisers, "What is it I should buy?" Perhaps they do.

Fear is the enemy—most of all, fear of largeness. The largeness of our own soul is most intimidating, which is why we defer so often to the instructions of others. When I see those hoards trooping into auditoriums and houses of worship to be told by coiffed gurus with limousines, even helicopters, what their values should be, and how they are to live their lives, I do not consider this "religion." I do not see a summons to the large risk of the soul or an enlarging encounter with mystery. I do not see such banalities honoring the gods and their terrible powers. I see it as an infantilizing repetition of the obligation of childhood to serve voices of outer authority, and it reinforces the recrudescent message that one's well-being derives from obeying the powerful

Other. The "Other" that also lies within us, the voice of our soul, seems, then, so impossibly far away.

Friedrich Nietzsche asserted in one of his oxymoronic aphorisms that we are an abyss, *and* we are the tightrope across the abyss. Tangentially, Martin Heidegger further observed that "the abyss is the openness of Being." When we bring these prophetic and provocative ideas together, we see that we are afraid of the largeness, the immense possibilities within ourselves. We all learned to run from the idea that the gods brought us here to carry out their will, whatever it may be, rather than serve the troubled timidity of our mutually neurotic communities. Yet, when we spin out our journey from our own deepest places, we find a continuity of intention, a steady feeling of support that allows us to cross over the abyss of our existential angst. Then we discover that what we feared most was our own terrible and insistent freedom.

Recently I wrote the following e-mail to an analysand who has gone through a difficult marital decision, experienced the abandonment of her religious community, the misunderstanding of her friends, and, despairing, is feeling horribly alone.

Dear _____:

This is the famous "dark night of the soul" described by St. John of the Cross centuries ago. Going through it is one requirement of an election in which suffering is the price of the ticket to rebirth. The collapse of the "false self" is painful indeed, but it is also how the Self begins to emerge from underneath all the attitudes and adaptations required in the past. This death/ rebirth, and this difficult "in-between," is how you get yourself back again, how you begin to bring who you are, really are, into this world. The former is in service to fear management, understandably; the latter is in service to Divinity.

You are a loving and lovable human being, and a great soul. Please try not to view your life through the caboose window of this rapidly moving train. You need to walk forward, enter the engine room, look out the window, and steer the thing ahead. The past is past, and is trailing behind us. The future, with new friends, relationships, and challenges, is rushing toward you, asking that you be ready for it. It will ask much of all of us, and we are summoned to be willing participants in the making of this future.

Choosing to risk one's own authority, to step into this fearful place, to realize through experience that one will be supported by something deep within each of us, is what brings us home to ourselves. After all, fear of largeness begins by fearing the resident largeness that is our own souls. If we can abide that fear of our ourselves, we will not be afraid of others. When I once expressed some apprehension before beginning an internship in a locked ward of a psychiatric hospital, my Zürich analyst said to me with Zen-like clarity, "When you have faced your own demons, the demons of others will not frighten you." I found that what he said was true. Within a few weeks there I was asked to do a workshop for the psychiatric staff. I organized the half day around the theme: *"How are you different from your patients here?"* I found that most of the staff said, in some version, "Well, they are crazy and I am not." I quickly learned that one of the ways that folks there defended themselves against the depth, complexity, and yes, craziness in themselves, was to split it off and deposit craziness only in the other. Facing our own abyss opens us to acceptance of the magnitude of the *other* as well, whether found in relationship, nature, or in the mysterious movement of the gods themselves.

Every day that we can call out those demons of fear and reductionism and step into the large journey intended by the soul, we actually serve the world better by bringing to it the unique gift that each of us represents. How could denying our gift to the world ever really serve it? Stepping into our largeness is not narcissism—it ultimately proves our greatest contribution to others. All it requires is the resolve to stand humbly but responsibly before our own largeness, and then to step into it.

Chapter Six

THAT WE RISK GROWTH OVER SECURITY

"You needn't fear what your life has meant,
You won't curse how your hours were spent."
"MAGDA GOEBBELS," W. D. SNODGRASS

*W*e have already established the fact that our common condition is fragile, perilous, and at the mercy of large powers and principalities over which we have no control. It would be logical, perhaps prudent, not to get out of bed in the morning.* In fact, whether we notice it or not, getting out of bed is an act of routinized habit, unwitting folly, or great courage. As an old proverb has it, knowing that one will not die of drowning does not save one from hanging, or a thousand other lethal rendezvous. In fact, if we look carefully at the foot of the bed, we will espy two little critters there—call them gremlins, call them demons. One is called *Fear*, and the other is called *Lethargy*. The former grins at us and shows its teeth, and the latter whispers sibilant seductions. The former says to us, in a most familiar way: "Hey, the world is too big for you, too scary, too powerful. Don't go out there, you'll

---

* The Snodgrass lines quoted above are meant ironically as Magda Goebbels, in the Führer bunker in Berlin, poisons her children in the final hours of the Reich. In the spent madness of her life, she rationalizes that she will spare her children such quiddities and reversals by killing them.

only get hurt. Don't show up." This is the cue for the latter, who whispers, "Hey . . ." (they really talk that way) "Hey . . . chill out, lie back, tomorrow's another day. Have a chocolate. Turn on the telly, hit the Internet, call Sally, pull the blanket back over your head." (Our world thoughtfully provides many, many virtual blankets to pull over consciousness and its difficult chores.)

In reality, they have a point. We do not get out of this business alive. We get hurt so easily. Living requires so much effort, sustained effort, and no one really helps or understands us anyway . . . or so, we say, reflexively, protectively, to ourselves . . . and all this in this first instant of summons to the day, all in the micro-moment of waking.

There *is* much to fear. Much too much is asked of us, and so it seems better not to show up. When I was a child, I heard such advice, such admonitions, literally, from very kind persons who were overwhelmed by life, battered, and defeated. So, they said, "Stay home . . . let us take care of each other . . . and by all means, don't go 'out there.' You will only get hurt, and get your heart broken." (Their fondest hope for me was that I would marry someone safe and predictable, live nearby, concur with their religious and cultural values, always wear clean underwear,* and work for Bell Telephone—a company that would be there in perpetuity, for after all, we will always have to make telephone calls, and Bell was clean and safe, compared to the assembly line of the tractor factory where my kin sweated out their lives amid flying steel shards, wearing steel shoes and shatterproof glasses.)

---

* I was commonly sent off to school with the specific admonition that my underwear had better be clean so that they would not be embarrassed if they had to come to the hospital to fetch me by day's end.

Actually they were very accurate in their assessment of their experience of life, and their admonitions were honest, loving, and protective.

Accordingly, for the first half of life, their well-meant advice pretty much dictated my biography. I left home for academe, fled one "mother complex"* for a collective mother complex, *alma mater*. I learned to intellectualize, stay above the fray, and to transcend ordinary planes of daily intercourse with reality. Still, life intrudes, one is hurt, one hurts others, and the heart is broken, however one tries to avoid it. At one critical moment, when I stood poised between my fears and my summons to a larger life, I asked myself a simple question: "Why, if you have done all the right things, did the assignment given you, do you feel so miserable inside?" I had a lovely family, a great job as a college professor, and a career track that offered an honorable security. So why, at age thirty-five, did I find myself in a dark wood?

This discrepancy between "the plan" and the ego's acquiescence to its instructions led me to my first hours of analysis. From those sessions, I realized that I was living someone else's life, their understandings, their sincerely felt beliefs. I had to find my own path through the dark wood, or die. From that therapy in America I felt called to go to the Jung Institute in Zürich, Switzerland, to pursue a deepened personal analysis and travel wherever it took me. Even so, so much internal traffic stood in the way of such a leap into the abyss of the unknown—most of all, the gremlin that

---

* By "mother complex," we are not considering the personal mother, but rather our common needs for security, familiarity, and belonging. These needs are hardly reprehensible, but when they prevail, make decisions for us, our summons to the rigor of life is subverted, and whatever we were meant to bring to the bigger picture is compromised.

danced at the foot of the bed and snarled: "You? You? You can't do that. It is too much for you. You will lose your home, your values, your family, your known points of reference."

Given that I was among the first of my extended family to graduate from high school, and the first to graduate from college, and the first to graduate from graduate school, this act was more than crossing the graduated series of Rubicons those steps had required. It was rather something as improbable as traveling to Mars. Nonetheless, I recall, and treasure, the day I left for college. My uncle Dale said, "Remember what the Bible said, Jimmy." "Huh?" I replied. "Whatsoever thy hand findeth to do, do with all thy might." I knew that in invoking Ecclesiastes, he was blessing my departure, though he did not know toward what distant shore I was traveling. His comment remains for me today a reminder, a blessing, and a mantra.

So, I asked myself another simple question: "What will it take to get to Zürich?" The passport was easy enough, the money borrowed was doable, the support and love of family was a given, but still the distant shore seemed too distant, and the task too large. So, what does it take to get to Zürich? As I pondered this conundrum one late hour, the answer came back to me as a clear voice: "You get on an airplane!" Well, even I knew the difference between the visit of a casual tourist and the risk of quite another kind of journey, but I also knew the truth of that compelling statement. Where did it come from? Was there some "other" there, or was it a hallucination? Intuitively, I knew, as we all do at some level, what I had to do. Going was dying, and staying was dying. When we get to junctures like that, we had better choose the dying that enlarges rather than the one that keeps us stuck.

One of the oldest of mythological motifs is that of the "dying god." In fact, I subsequently wrote my thesis on that subject at the Jung Institute. The dying-god motif can be found in virtually all of the ancient religions and mythologies, especially those of the Mediterranean and the Levant, not the least of which is the paradox central to Christianity. Logically this oxymoron seems a contradiction. How can a *god* die? Is not a *god* an Immortal? What this archetypal motif suggests is that when certain principles, energies, values are denied, or have been pushed to exhaustion, they cease to function as sources of vitality. Yet, in the underworld, they grow and reemerge in some new form, and the cycle is renewed. This macro-cosmic pattern is played out in the seasons, of course, and in the cycles of civilizations, but also in the micro-developmental patterns of each of us.

Our moral, intellectual, and emotional development embodies a series of deaths, followed by enlargements of soul often painfully acquired. It was once scary to leave home and walk all the way to school by ourselves. It was scary to leave Mom and Dad and venture out into the adult world on our own. It remains scary to lose a marriage, have the children leave, lose friends, lose old dependencies and verities we took for granted, lose our youth, and finally, it remains scary to lose our life. Yet all of these deaths are driven by our nature, by the deep forces that course through us, and have so driven our stories from the beginning of time. Through analysis I learned that something in me had to die before the rest of me, the larger part, could live. My acquired selfhood had to pass before a larger engagement with the Self was possible.

One of my thesis examiners—a woman who was perhaps sixty at the time (I was forty-two)—said during the thesis defense, "I didn't begin to individuate until my god died." She spoke with quiet solemnity and all of us nodded, knowingly, because all of us had gone through many deaths to reach that place in our spiritual geographies. In every "death" we had to decide whether we were going to fold the cards, put the chairs away, and die, or die unto the old world and step into the scary new world. Either way, death was the only choice. No wonder we so often choose security over growth, or try to stay as unconscious of our summons as we can. We have an entire culture of addictive treatment plans, of sensate distraction, and of jejune impatience that is driven by the preference of security through unconsciousness as an antidote to growth.

In my first dream in Zürich, which I dutifully brought to my new analyst, I was—imagine this—a knight on the ramparts of a medieval castle. The castle was under siege. The air was thick with clouds of arrows flying in my direction. At the edge of the forest I could see that a witch-like figure was directing the assault. As the dream ended I was consumed with anxiety and the very real question of whether the castle would hold. Is that not a classic midlife dream, and even more, a beginning of analysis dream?

The "knight" is my armored ego, stoutly defending conscious attitudes. The "castle" is the self-constructed world and the defensive perimeter against whatever opposition arises. After all, wasn't this the message of the family of origin—"stay at home, fortify the walls, it is too dangerous out there. Don't leave your castle; you will only get pounded and your heart broken." And they weren't wrong. Yet that same castle asks a death of us as well, the death that too much security exacts from our journeys. And was not that witchy presence an outcry from my alienated, distanced anima?

Upon receiving the dream, my Swiss analyst, Dr. Adolf Ammann, said to me, "You will have to lower the drawbridge and go out and meet her and find out why she is so hostile." "Yeah . . . right," I thought. "She means me no good," I did say. But, in for a penny, in for a pound, and so I began the process of leaving Castle Securitas for the Journey Perilous, and in so doing engaging the other parts of my psyche, which had grown estranged and rather testily opinionated. In choosing security over growth, we all outrage the soul, and the soul, outraged, manifests in symptoms—depression, anxiety disorders, envy and jealousy of others, dependencies, and so many more.

Shortly after that, I had my second dream. I was outside the German village of Berchtesgaden (where we had in fact recently visited, and walked those portions of the underground Führer bunker that survived Allied explosives). I realized that I had lost my eight-year-old son in that underground labyrinth. Pause with that image: to lose one's child in the labyrinthine underground. Naturally, as any parent would, I panicked and began to search, fruitlessly. I then ran into the village to the office of the burgomaster, to the local parson, to the schoolhouse, even the fire department, but no one would or could help find my child. Disconsolately, I wandered into the forest where I encountered a man who said he was Urgus—bearded and disheveled, his torso was rugged, and his legs grew into the ground—and added that he would help me find my child. (*Ur* is the German prefix for primal or original, and *gus* suggested to me something of my unmet Swedish grandfather, Gustav Lindgren.) This engagement with the primal, archaic masculine energy was both numinous—for I knew he spoke the truth—and intimidating, for I knew Urgus would ask much of me. Nonetheless, this encounter with the split-off, archaic masculine was the beginning of a journey of another kind, asking a different kind of death, and a progressive loss of security.

I had one last dream. I was back in the United States, teaching in a familiar classroom, except that the backside of this classroom was a canebrake, behind which was a jungle. From this jungle a person whom I had not seen since childhood emerged. He strode forth, grabbed me by the neck and lifted me off the ground with one arm. I found his intrusion frightening and humiliating. He spoke one sentence before dropping me and striding back off into that jungle: "I just want you to know who is really in charge here!"

Here was another death, the death of the falsely constructed academic, rational self. This constructed self was valuable in many settings, but as a defense against the archaic and anarchic feelings left behind in childhood, was now an impediment. In fact, one of the most profound truths I learned from that process in Zürich was that *what we have become is frequently the chief obstacle to our journey.* What we have become is typically an assemblage of defense mechanisms and anxiety-management systems generated by the adaptive needs that our fate-fueled biographies bring to us.

This ominous figure, whom I had not seen since childhood, was in reality named Leroy Solomon (*le Roi Solomon*), or King Solomon. He embodied my native wisdom, my native strength, and he wanted to confront and overthrow my assembled defenses and pull me out of the protective "mother complex"—that is, the choice to stay safe rather than grow up.

Who would ever make these dream images and scenarios up? What immense wisdom lies within each of us, what astonishing symbol-forming energies, and in service to what insistent summons to the journey do these images bring us? I am still amazed by these three initial dreams, their wisdom, their imperative, and their undeniable challenge to me.

For each of us a perilous Symplegades confronts us each day, whether we make our conflicts conscious or not. The Symplegades are the clashing rocks through which Homer's heroes must steer their fragile barks on their journeys home. Each day we are summoned to steer between fear and lethargy, and to find our narrow passage onward. Recently I was doing a radio interview in connection with a previous book when I mentioned that the majority of clients I see in analysis are between fifty and seventy-five years old. The interviewer, well educated and informed, said, "But we were told in grad school that old people really didn't change, that they were locked in." I replied that when she and/or her instructors were somewhat older they might have a different attitude.

Yes, we all know people who have died long before their bodies fell to earth. The world is full of people droning on, sitting before the telly or the Internet, waiting to die, living only for small sensations of scandal or vicarious catastrophe that they can witness from afar. But my experience of working with people, and I am sure that of my colleagues, is that the human psyche continues to ask us to grow, to develop, to explore, to be curious. Boredom is the pathology of the depressed, or the unimaginative. Ceasing to grow is a failure of nerve, because it is not what our psyche demands.

There is so much more to learn, to experience, to develop in our talents, curiosities, and explorations. Our enemies are the same old familiar gremlins: fear and lethargy. What makes Odysseus a hero to us, a prototype of our journey, is that he is willing to face his fears and persist, always persist. In his greatest peril he says, "I will stay with it and endure though suffering hardship, and once the heaving sea has shaken my raft to pieces, then will I swim."*

So often when he and his crew arrive at the various isles of respite, with their sundry seductions or fractious fears, Homer tells us, "and they forgot the journey." Getting intimidated or distracted is common enough. It happens to all of us. But when these diversions from our separate developmental imperatives prevail, we lose our journey, lose our life, and violate the intention of the gods in bringing us here.

Jung observed that we endeavor to educate our young, but do not educate our forty-year-olds about the task of the second half of life. If the first half is in service to an essentially social agenda, namely, the task of developing sufficient ego strength to leave parents, sortie into the world, commit to obligations, partner up, serve citizenship roles, then what is the task of the second half? Just a century ago, the average age of mortality was roughly forty-seven, so many of the readers of this book, statistically, would not be here, including the author. Also, in that era, social-role expectations, particularly gender constructs, were so compelling, so nor-

---

* *The Odyssey*, V, l. 363. (I have this reminder taped to the printer of my computer in my office.)

mative, that most people pretty much had their script laid out for them. To survive within such scripts was one thing, but to depart from those consensual definitions of identity was usually worse—to experience exile.

When we ask what value we serve in the second half of life, perhaps having contributed already to the commonweal, perhaps having helped reproduce the species, we suspect that we are not just here to kill time, hang out, pay taxes, receive benefits, and then die. Admittedly, after one has labored and sacrificed to achieve one's small purchase on security—one's home, family, identity, retirement—why would one risk losing it? It is easy to prattle on about the journey, but in the world of daily struggle and achievement, why should one throw these modest securities away? This practical objection makes perfect sense, but for one thing: Our psyche, our soul, wants something more of us, *through* us, and won't stop insisting.

Virtually everyone who comes to me in therapy has an achieved life with its usual disappointments, yet apparently something more is asked of them, and its neglect manifests in their depressions, dreams, addictions, and disquietudes. They, too, did all the right things, by the best lights of their consciousness, but their psyches rebelled nonetheless.

One man expressed it this way: "I always sought to win whatever the game was, and only now do I realize how much I have been played by the game. I played the game hard and willingly, always thinking I was winning something. But in the end there really was nothing to win, or what I did win really didn't matter in the end." How eloquently his words describe the discoveries of so many of us. While this insight is hardly new, we all have to discover it in our own ways before we believe it. Go back and reread Ecclesiastes, written millennia ago. Our brother there describes how his projections also fell on riches, achievement, sundry other expectations, and in the end he found them all *hebel*, or "mist." We all set off expecting the achievement of our goals to bring lasting satisfaction. It is not that the goals are unworthy, as such, but that they so often become tempting stopping places for the soul, places where we decline the invitation to trade still more mystery for security.

Or consider the woman who, at age fifty, after her second marriage went south, said, "I always thought my marriage would define me, *be* me. I know now I was never even *me* in those marriages, or any other relationships." Who she was, and what her journey was, became thereafter the conscious vector for our work together. The story of these two persons is the story of virtually all of us, if we stop and think about it. Where do we go in the second half of life, and in service to what?

The second half of life is a summons to the life of the spirit, namely, to ask, and answer for ourselves, uniquely, separately, *what matters most*. When we resist the many deaths asked of us, we resist the summons into larger life. When we resist engaging our fears in service to growth, we abrogate the will of the gods. The poet Rainer Maria Rilke said it best when he asserted that *our task is to be defeated by ever-larger things*. While the youthful ego can scarcely countenance defeat, the mature, second-half-of-life person knows that life is a series of continuing defeats, especially for the delusions of ego sovereignty. To be defeated by ever-larger things is indeed our task, for that means that we are growing, growing, growing. As playwright Christopher

Fry put it in *A Sleep of Prisoners*, this summons is upon us, "never to leave us till we take / the longest stride of soul men ever took. / Affairs are now soul size. / The enterprise is exploration into God."

Once we realize that affairs are soul-sized, then we realize that our familiar companions, fear and lethargy, cannot be permitted to prevail, lest our lives be a waste and our souls disdained. Every day the decision comes back to us: Choose growth or security—you cannot have both. Steer your frail bark between the clashing Symplegades, die unto the blandishments of fear and lethargy, and sail on, or slip back into harbor, unpack your precious cargo, and die.

◆   ◆   ◆

Recently, a very thoughtful analysand said, "I came here to analysis to find answers, and all you have done is show me more and more questions."

I concurred with his chagrined assessment.

He said that he had come searching for a resolution to his uncertainties. Among other things, he wanted a guru. After all, if I did not possess, and for a fee would not provide, answers for his existential anxieties, what would treat them? What had I learned along the Dharma Road that would address his disquietude?

He was right again in his assessment, and insistent on his intent to find Truth.

I said, "But I *have* answered your questions. You asked *what mattered most*; you asked how to live your life; and you asked what the answer to all these questions is."

"But what is it?"

"I taught you *to be more comfortable with your uncertainty.*" That is the answer. I added, "Any other answer that was *my* answer would, in the end, prove not to be *your* answer, or, if *your* answer, or any 'answer' at all, would prove over time to be limited, outgrown, constricting."

He nodded, and understood.

We are not here to be comfortable, although that is the banal blandishment offered by modern materialism, pop psychologies and theologies,* and the sundry seductions of addiction and distraction. "In the end, I taught you to be more comfortable in your uncertainty. This acceptance of ambiguity will better lead you to a more developmental agenda, a mystery-driven life, than 'certainty' ever would."

He agreed. And now he is truly on the Dharma Road.

---

* I know of one area "Christian" church that does not have a cross inside because, reportedly, "It might make people uncomfortable." Apparently, no one therein has read Dietrich Bonhoeffer's *The Cost of Discipleship*, or heard of the oxymoron "cheap grace," or perhaps paid very much attention to the originator of their faith, who made a lot of folks uncomfortable.

Chapter Seven

THAT WE LIVE VERBS
NOT NOUNS

"Signatures of all things I am here to read, seaspawn and
seawrack, the nearing tide."
JAMES JOYCE, *ULYSSES*

$\mathcal{L}$et us recall for a moment that our ego—which seems
to us our center, our core, our identity, our rock of ages—is
itself one "complex" among many. It is the central complex
of consciousness—*who we think we are* at any given moment, but in any given moment that "complex," malleable as
it is, may be subsumed by other energies with quite contrary
agendas, scripts, and provisional identities, and together they
collusively produce unpredictable outcomes. (As anyone
knows who looks soberly at his or her accumulated history.)
Swimming in such frangible murk, the ego naturally has a
preference for certainty over uncertainty, predictability over
surprise, clarity over ambiguity, control over anarchy, decision over ambivalence, and so on. Thus, this Nervous Nellie
ego flits about trying to make everything work, slapping her
head, boxing her neighbors, obsessed with staying in charge.
As part of her agitated agenda, Nellie seeks to live in a world
of nouns, comforting nouns, that is, fixed identities, coun-
ters on a table to be moved at will, predictable entities that

can be controlled, maneuvered, and contained. And all the while, Nellie really swims in a sea of verbs. That is, not *things fixed*, but *things happening*. And Nellie, tripping over this fact from time to time, grows all the more unsettled, anxious, kerfluffled, and flits about even more.

All of us carry fixed, reified assumptions about the nature of reality. Once people believed that there was an afterlife "up there"—Heaven—or "down there"—Hell. They believed the testimony of their ordinary senses and thus lived in a three-story universe. Moreover, they embraced a flattering picture of our Earth that proudly stood, like the ego, at the center of all things. (If you doubt Nellie's agitation, and her resolve to "fixate" things, render them stable, predictable, just remember Bruno immolated for suggesting otherwise, Galileo under house arrest by the Red Guard of his time for the crime of presenting an alternative picture in which this Earth is relegated to a planet only, circling about a sun, one of millions of suns, as we now know. For their dethronement of Nellie's ego fantasy of sovereignty, stability, fixity, such men would burn.)

Centuries later, in a slightly more tolerant time, Freud proudly proclaimed his vision as the third great revolution in human self-conception. The first dethronement of the human ego was launched by the Copernican revolution, of which Bruno and Galileo were a part, in which Nellie's egoistic hubris was relocated in a much vaster, more impersonal system of swirling galaxies. The second profound revolution was wrought by Charles Darwin, in which the uniqueness of this species, and its anthropocentric creation, are revisioned as a part of a long developmental journey over millions of years, a journey yet unfinished. (To this day it is amazing that ostensibly educated persons would deny this dynamic process when we can see evolution occurring in real time in our finite lives as we grow, change, adapt to new dietary and health conditions, develop immunities to antibiotics, and so on. Evolutionary process is occurring in each moment of our being.)* The third great revolution Freud modestly claimed for himself in his identification of the immensity and power of the unconscious, upon which the ego floated like an iceberg, with only a fragment above surface and, coursing through tenebrous inner seas, an unchartable immensity below.

These three revisionings of our locus in time and space were stoutly resisted by the vested authorities of each era in which they were articulated. They are still being resisted by those Nervous Nellies who pack school boards to control teachers, syllabi, and a body of knowledge they scarcely understand, shunning an accumulation of learning acquired painstakingly by specialists in each field. The natural curiosity and intelligence of those whom they would protect are insulted, diminished. Because of their fears, their own children are rendered less competitive in the world by restricting their access to the best information and rigorously tested theory that is increasingly part of our common world treasure. Such is the power of Nellie's fear, such the power of weak egos to resist any affront to their sovereignty, such the timidity of soul that

---

* For example, modern genetics, the "floor plan" of our being, is now seen not in the Mendelean view of the nineteenth century as a fixed code, but as a continuously evolving, interactive system through which the exigencies of environmental conditions, and the reactions of inner psychological life, are absorbed, reconstrued, and recombined in a continuous dialogue between our outer and inner worlds. Recent reports have indicated that our changes are accelerating, and that we are evolving, as measured by our DNA markers, at a rate one hundred times faster than that of our grandparents.

abhors ambiguity, challenge, and genuine dialogue with the "otherness" of the other. Such Nellies not only restrict the flow of ideas, they garrison themselves in psychological, spiritual, and political fortresses against their enemies—change, ambiguity, the complex, the unknown—enemies who have already stormed their gates and occupied their psychic citadels. They would not defend so stoutly if they did not harbor secret doubts themselves.

Gertrude Stein once said of Oakland, California, no doubt unfairly, "there is no *there*, there." We now know there is no "up there," there. Yet most people still operate with an archaic world view, an antiquated cosmic picture, despite the simple fact that if the resurrected Jesus were literally propelled "up" or "out there," his body would still be trackable by current telemetry. That the idea of "resurrection" might mean something else entirely seems too threatening to those who are "metaphor challenged." (As one woman said to me, "I got turned off of all that church stuff. And I never understood the idea of "resurrection" until I attended my first AA meeting." Her "resurrection" has not spared her suffering since, but it has led her to the most empowered phase of her life thus far.)

It is our natural tendency—within me as much as the next person—to want to reify, fix, harden, locate the world, and pin it down, in order to control it. As natural as this need is, it may also be the chief source of our misunderstanding, our alienation from the world and from the mysterious energies that inform it. Nowhere is this tendency to domination greater than in the Western world. We have gained great sovereignty over our natural environment, but seem more and more uprooted and unhappy all the time.

The classical Eastern view that all is in flux, that the point is to be present to the present, and to "go with the flow," is a tempting but bitter pill for us to swallow. Twenty-six centuries ago, the pre-Socratic philosopher Heraclitus observed that "all is fire," by which he meant, metaphorically, all is in flux. He further famously asserted that we cannot step twice into the same stream, for the second time the stream has flowed onward, and we have flowed onward as well. Nevertheless, even Plato, one of the pioneers of metaphysics, sought to find or construct a permanent reality, a ground of fixed being, and plaintively petitioned, "Bring me that person who can show me the One from amid the many and I will hold him to my heart's core." In the movement from Heraclitus to Plato, the ego is strengthened, the Western world launched in earnest, and our estrangement from this verbing universe of "ten thousand passing things" deepened, an abyss that continues to yawn the more we make "progress."

THE OLDEST OF RELIGIOUS HERESIES

When we consider how a religious idea emerges in the first place, we must recall that it never begins as an "idea." It occurs as a highly charged, affective *experience of transcendence*, and later, much later, becomes an idea. For example, a small group bands together for security, division of labor, increase of the gene pool, whatever reason. So formed, they are a *society*. A society is here to serve a purpose. Societies are horizontally structured, and driven by conscious purpose(s). When the purpose changes, or when other forces grow more powerful, the society dissolves. Only when such a group experiences the vertical do they become a *community*. This vertical vector, be it incarnated in a prophet, a natural event, a sociopolitical moment, lifts each individual up and out of his or her sack of skin into an imaginal, collective experience. Communities, thus connected to a transcendent experience, have more psychological staying power than societies.

Whatever form the transcendent experience presents, an "image" emerges from it. In other words, an invisible, felt, psychologically compelling experience is embodied, incarnated in some preternatural image—be it a burning bush, a charismatic prophet, a great battle, or a migration. For those who were part of the original event, that image need not be "explained," because it is still able to point beyond itself and reconnect with the felt reality of the primal experience. Such an effectively and affectively charged image is a *symbol*.

When an image wanes in its power to point beyond itself, to summon up a compelling affective response to the original, it devolves into a *sign*. *A symbol points toward mystery; a sign denotes a content, an "idea."* As people begin to experience the image as a content, they also suffer a progressive discrepancy between the image and the affect it was once able to evoke. In response to this progressive devolution of any image, humankind has created three forms whose purpose is to retain access to, transmit the meaning of, and bind the community to its original encounter and its communal meaning. These three retentive forms are *dogma, rites*, and *cultic* practices.

Dogma formulates the questions and putative answers to whatever "meaning" has arisen from or been ascribed to the primal encounter. What happened? From whence did it come? What does it mean to us? What does it ask of us? These and other questions are meant to satisfy the mind when the original affective power of the encounter has already begun to wane.* In time, of course, dogma can cease to summon any affect, and then grows dry, sterile, and, well . . . dogmatic.

Rites evolve as reenactments of primal experience in the hope of recapturing its original numinosity. They, too, can in time seem arbitrary and disconnected. "So, why is it that we do this rite each year?" "Well . . . because we always have." "Oh . . ."

Cultic practices—how we prepare our food, marry, bury our dead, develop ethical and juridical systems, and so on—are means by which one differentiates those who had primal encounter X rather than encounters Y and Z. These quite elaborate and unique expressions always claim their sanction from divine origin, or ancestral authority, and provide community members a sense of belonging and attachment networks, and help preserve received sets of values. So, religions, nations, ethnic groups cheer for their team, wear purple and gold, or some other set of colors, and go "rah, rah!" when their team is on the field of play. Here, too, such cultic differences prove arbitrary and quaint over time, although they remain "our team" and evoke nostalgic identifications and militant defenses.

What happens to community, once organized around a felt encounter with the transcendent, is that it gets institutionalized. Institutions serve many defensible purposes, especially the maintenance and transmission of particular values.

---

* Analogously, Harry Slochower argues in his fine book, *Mythopoesis*, a study of the classics of the Western world, *Don Quixote*, *Faust*, Dostoyevsky, Thomas Mann, and others, that a writer acts to preserve the story, and its mythic values, just when its power over the collective imagination has already begun to recede.

Yet, as we know, institutions so often have a peculiar way of ending up violating the principles of their founding. Seemingly, two inherent laws of institutions invariably emerge: first, they preserve the institution at all costs, even at the risk of selectively compromising their founding vision,* and second, they preserve the status of their priesthood, whether they be clerics with vested authority, executives with golden parachutes, academics with rank and tenure, or politicians who change the laws to privilege their kind. Institutions, necessary as they are, cast a long shadow of self-interest, and typically end up severing the affective connection to their founding experiences and generative values.

So, too, we reify whatever image arises spontaneously from the primal encounter. The *phenomenon* is the felt experience of the image, charged with sufficient affect to move us, shake us, perhaps terrify us. The *epiphenomenon* is what we make of that image, how we understand it, communicate it, later perhaps institutionalize it. Remember that the transcendent office of a symbol is to point beyond itself to the primal Other. When this imaged aperture into the timeless still works, we stand for a while in relationship with genuine mystery. However, our egos are uncomfortable with that profound otherness and tend to move the experience from a verb—that is, *something happening*—to something that happened, to move it from a phenomenologically felt encounter to an object that we can understand, perhaps control. In

---

* One example of many may be found in the shift of a major U.S. denomination from affirming Christ as the source of their authority to that of the Bible. Apparently the former hung out with embarrassing types, broke down too many barriers between people, while the latter offers enough scattered, tribal opinion to allow anyone to legitimize his complexes, prejudices, and special interests.

those moments we risk the oldest of religious heresies, namely, *idolatry.*

Albeit unwittingly, we all are idolaters, for from time to time we grow bewitched by our constructs, and are seduced by our need for fixity over intelligence. Let me give you three very practical examples. Some years ago I was listening to NPR on the car radio as the journalist Murray Kempton was being interviewed. He told of flying to Memphis to interview Martin Luther King during the height of the civil rights struggles. At the airport he got in a taxi and told the driver to take him to the church of Dr. Martin Luther King. The taxi driver refused to budge. "All right, then," Kempton added, "take me to the church of the *alleged* Dr. Martin Luther King." The taxi roared off toward Ebenezer Baptist Church. Similarly, a "faith-based" community agency, devoted to educating minority children, "fired" a popular and admittedly effective teacher because she legally changed her comfortable name to something possibly identified with another religious tradition. So much for toleration, preparing children who have to function in this world as it really is, and the liberating value of diversity. Third, two years before the presidential campaign actually began, I saw an e-mail from a person in a leadership position of a prominent nonprofit ominously warning staff and others against the possible candidacy of Senator Barack Obama because his name *sounds* like Osama bin Laden. That this worthy, highly educated and privileged, is so easily spooked by paradigm shift, and so meretriciously resorts to spurious analogy, reminds us that fear of change often overwhelms our higher selves and professed principles. Each of these examples reveals the tendency of the insecure to be easily unsettled, and to prefer idolatrous seduction by nouns rather than romancing the ambiguity of verbs. Sadly, "the better angels of our nature," to use Lincoln's phrase from his first inaugural speech, are too easily trumped by the lethal combination of fear and ignorance.

Idolatry occurs when the focus of our affective commitment has shifted from the primal Other to the image itself. When, for example, the various prophets of the Bible inveigh against worshipping graven images of all kinds, they offer profound respect for the mystery that can never be contained within an image. While ego consciousness wishes images upon which to fasten, such images betray the mystery, isolate it, limit it, and therefore move from the world of verbs to the world of nouns. Theologian Paul Tillich once noted that *God* is the God who appears from out behind the God who disappeared. In other words, the mystery that courses through the universe refuses to be contained in our *imago Dei*, so it leaves it behind as a mere image and artifact of consciousness, and reemerges in a new form just when consciousness begins to take it for granted.

Another example may help. The etymology of the name *Zeus* means "the lightening." Zeus is not the sun, nor synonymous with the sun, but rather the moment when the darkness is pierced by the first rays of the sun. Zeus is not the gaseous ball in the sky but rather the moving experience of being suffused with light. Zeus, then, is an aperture into wonder. Later, Zeus is construed a personage, with certain attributes, certain personality characteristics, and morphs in time into something suspiciously like us. In fact, all the gods, first experienced as Wholly Other, to use theologian Karl Barth's term, transform slowly into arbitrary parental figures, jealous uncles, contentious cousins, nagging mothers-in-law, and so on. They receive the imprint of our projections, our limited ways of appropriating divinity, which by definition wholly transcends our petty conceptual apparatus. In short, the verbs that charge the universe—angry Ares, the power of rage; alluring Aphrodite, the ineluctable summons to love; aesthetic Apollo, the enticing arc of the graceful; hearty Hephaestus, the tool-wielding smith—all that goodly company become nouns, mere biographies, and, over time, lose their numinosity. A god without mojo is dead, no matter how many priests, no matter how many parishioners, no matter how institutionally formidable.

When the form is worshipped, the god is "dead"—that is, the energic mystery that gave it life is supplanted by a human construct. This is what Friedrich Nietzsche meant in the nineteenth century when he said that God was dead. He was not making a metaphysical statement, nor even a theological pronouncement; he was observing a psychological fact that the souls of his contemporaries were devoted to the forms of worship and not to engaging that continuously transforming Other that confounds all formulae and ego-bewitchments.* Similarly, the Danish theologian Søren Kierkegaard reminded his contemporaries that the god that can be named is not God; it has become an artifact of ordinary consciousness, and thereby is about *us*, not about mystery.** A more recent, prescient soul is the

---

* Nietzsche added that he could worship only a dancing god, namely, a verbing encounter, not a dead noun.

** Jung once asserted that "every psychology is a subjective confession." What, then, can be said of most of our psychologies is that they reveal our ego-driven fantasy of control, management, and narcissistic comfort. If our psychologies are thus devoted to the banal, rather than the mystery of the soul, and the psyche's infinite depths, what then of our contemporary theologies?

Episcopal Bishop John Shelby Spong, who writes of a professor of theology who told him, " 'Any God who can be killed ought to be killed. . . .' We also need to face the fact that any deity who must be protected from truth, arising from any source, has died already."*

A man with whom I am now working had this dream recently. His outer context is that he is nearing retirement, yet wishes to grow psychologically and spiritually while recognizing a deep need for community and companionship outside his good marriage. For some time he sought this companionship within his professional peers, but found that his questions have moved him beyond whatever brought them together in the first place. Additionally, he sought companionship with other men in his church group. But once again he finds that the larger questions he has opened to have moved him beyond simple Bible study, geared to find "answers," and then conform to "answers," which ostensibly satisfied others from another time, another place. He realizes that such self-professed "study" is not truly developmental, not even really spiritual, but rather an effort to combat doubt, avoid honest inquiry, and finesse ambiguity by embracing a received, external authority.

So, here is his dream, which encapsulates both the issue and the resolution:

> I am at a Sunday school class sitting around a circular table with six or seven other men. I have the sense that the fellow next to me is wanting me to get into the whole Bible study thing. As we start talking as a group, I say, "Yes,

* John Shelby Spong, *Jesus for the Non-Religious*, p. xii.

Christ is the current of light in the center of the table."
My saying this seems to ruin the whole meeting and the
guy to the right of me is crying and I feel bad. Nonetheless, I say again, "Yes, Christ is the current in the center of
the table." Again the guy is crying and everybody looks
upset, as if I've just taken a crap in Bible study class. I decide to leave, feeling confused as if I have ruined something for others. I don't understand why they don't
understand what I was saying. And I really don't see why
this comment would be so troubling to them.

This dream is very close to the actual feelings he has
been having in his group. His spontaneous observation
threatens the group, for they are not interested in exploration
but in finding certainty, less concerned about enlargement
through personal, original insight than the more secure validation of external authority. If we see the weeping man as an
aspect of the dreamer, we realize that he, too, laments a simpler past, but like Bruno and Galileo, he cannot unsee what
he has seen for himself. And the dream gets it right. It is a
profound theological commentary upon what opens him to
the heart of mystery. As the dream rightly asks, why should
the simple pursuit of the ever more complex be so troubling?
How does this man who wishes to affirm his tradition find
an understanding consistent with his education, his reason,
his respect for complexity?

Jesus was a man imbued with all the gifts and short-
comings of the human condition, including mortality. *If*
he was the Christ, the anointed one, the messiah, then he
was also something else—namely, the carrier of a divine energy. Consider this: We all respect, profit from, and utilize

lightbulbs. But we do not worship the glass bulb, the humble vessel. It is the energy that inhabits it, invests through it, that brings light into our darkness. It is not Gautama who is luminous, but he serves as the vehicle through which the rays of enlightenment shine. As the old Zen saying has it, "If you meet the Buddha on the road, kill him." That is, the Buddha is a symbol of our universal potential for enlightenment, for seeing through,* and to worship the person is to miss the whole point. It is not the bulb, it is the energy that charges, that renders the bulb luminous.

So this dreamer knows consciously that his search for companions on the road is frustrated for now, for most of those he encounters are not on the road at all, but lodged at comfort stations along the way. He understands that the Jesus of history may have in fact embodied luminosity, numinosity, and deeply moved others. What is divine, of course, is not the earthly husk of Jesus, or any of us, but what shines through us into this dark world. *Christ* is not someone's name, not a noun, a fixed dogma or practice, but an energy, a current among many currents, which together and separately enact the mystery we call divine. The gods are not nouns, but verbs.

Intrapsychically, we all get stuck at way stations on our journey—prior understandings of ourselves, presumptive contracts with the gods, dependent roles, archaic expectations imposed on others. Our own psyche is forever coursing forward, destroying the old, moving dialectically toward the unknown, but we all tend to fight this process. Many

---

* The Sanskrit verb *budh* means "to see"—in other words, to see *through* the delusions of the ego to the essential energic nature of being, which is never static but forever transforming.

persons whom I see in therapy arrive finally for this humbling appointment with themselves because they resisted such growth until their psyches revolted in irrepressible pathologies. What our ego resists will persist. Either way we are called to "die" unto the old. Either we die unto who we were, in order to move to the next stage, or we die through staying stuck, and suffer stasis and stultification. Jeanine will not let go of the fantasy that someone will fix it for her; Karen will not grow up; George will not face his fear of conflict and thus remains a good boy. Each of them is stuck in a reified world, a world of nouns, even as the verbing world slips the secure platform from beneath their feet the more they try to stand pat.

Do not all of us resist change, fearing what may follow the familiar? Do we not resist the ample evidence that the only thing constant is change? Do we not, even in the face of personal precedent and the testimony of all of the great world religions, oppose our own developmental stages, especially our aging and inexorable drift toward dissolution? Is not our chief neurosis—by which I mean estrangement from nature—our desire to hold fast to what is forever transforming, to freeze the familiar, to submit motion to stasis, to solicit immortality through reification and rigidity?

Still one other person who illustrates this paradoxical relationship between verbs and nouns is the nineteenth-century Jesuit priest Gerard Manley Hopkins (1844–1889) in many of his richly metaphoric struggles with mystery. He both believed and doubted with equal conscientious fervor. That his struggle remained unresolved, that he expressed both praise and doubt, that he gloried in his Creator and walked alone through the dark night of the soul, is continuing testimony to the authenticity of his spiritual journey. Among his most illustrative engagements between nouns and verbs is his gorgeous poem "That Nature is a Heraclitean Fire and of the Comfort of the Resurrection." Even in the mud beneath our feet he sees Divinity, Divinity verbing:

> *Squandering ooze to squeezed dough, crust, dust; stanches, starches*
> *Squadroned masks and manmarks treadmill toil there*
> *Footfretted in it. Million-fueled, nature's bonfire burns on . . .*

There is Heraclitus—"nature's bonfire"—returned. Hopkins's wonder-terror at the evanescence of this godly "verbing" leads him to embrace the paradox of resurrection, that death is only the end of a noun, but whatever energizes that noun we call ourselves transforms into something even more mysterious.

Thus, even in this carbonized, organic paste on a jocund frame of bones that we are, Hopkins sees Divinity at work, transforming, transforming . . . and is stunned to find his own mortal but bejeweled place in a profoundly verbing universe:

> *This Jack, joke, poor potsherd, patch, matchwood, immortal diamond,*
> *Is immortal diamond.*

In the end, Hopkins is a religious poet not because he is a priest who writes poetry, nor because he takes up "religious" themes, but because he knows that the Mystery is a verb, not a noun. His Jesus is a noun, a biographical event. His Christ is a verb, coursing through history as an archetypal energy driving toward wholeness, cruciforming to where history and transcendence converge. It is a matter of personal conviction whether or not one subscribes to a particular mythic narrative, but it is our common story that we, these current carriers of mystery, are merely nouns in our conscious lives, but in our journey through time and space we are all verbs. Both modern science and the intuitions of a village priest converge in this paradox of our star-driven journey whereby we as mere carbon are nouns, but as energized carbon are gerunds—verbing, verbing, always verbing. . . .

Chapter Eight

That We Find and Follow the Path of Creativity and Delight in Foolish Passions

*"What if you slept, and what if in your sleep you dreamed, and
what if in your dream you went to heaven and there plucked a
strange and beautiful flower, and what if when you awoke you had
the flower in your hand? Ah, what then?"*
    Samuel Taylor Coleridge

*"Man cannot tarry long in a state of consciousness; he must
retire again into the unconscious, for that is where his roots are."*
    Paul Klee, *Farbenlehre*

*J*ust this morning I was with a man who practices a very
serious profession in a very serious way with a lifelong commitment to justice, social equity, and to making his community a better place to live. In the midst of our session he
made a very serious confession, an admission of sorts, and
waited for a reaction. He confessed . . . are you ready for this?
He confessed that in the last eighteen months he had become an *oenophile!* Yes, it was a humbling confession that
he had come to love, be fascinated by, the cultivation of

grapes, the process through which they are nurtured, harvested, treated, and the mysterious elixir that may or may not result from this alchemical process. In short, gasp . . . he had become a lover of the cultivation and delectation of wines!

So what is the problem here?

In his value system, with all its emphasis on right values, right work, right vocation, being an oenophile felt like an indulgence, an affectation. He associated oenophilia with snobbery, with excess money, and with idleness. Perhaps this vinous enthusiasm is embodied by some who fit this description, but not this man. What he is suffering at the moment is the gulf between what Freud called the "Over-I" (*Über-Ich/* Super-Ego) and the "It-ness of his nature" (*Das Es,* the Id, the It). But it seems that something of his nature insisted, and forced a natural enthusiasm to the surface, despite his considered, and considerably refined, moral reservations.

Perhaps with equal perversity,* pandas animate the "foolish passion" of a close friend. She literally travels the world to visit them, daily feasts on live Internet feeds from various zoos, and has formed many distant friendships through this common passion. Pandas speak to something deep within her, and such moments are to be honored. Something within each of us is stirred by forms, images, values, to which others may prove indifferent or incredulous. If such images and forms speak to us, occasion *resonance*, then they express in outer form some analogue to what lies within. To those things that do not resonate within

---

* *Perversity* means to turn away from the norm, to be original, to experiment, not to be confused with *perversion.*

us, we are indifferent, no matter what the endorsement by fashion, popular taste, or vested authority. Such stirring within must be respected, for it is a movement of soul whose vagaries can never nor should be subsumed by mere practicality.

One of the most risible book titles I ever encountered was, as best I distantly, inaccurately remembered from the graduate school shelves, *On the Outbreak of Enthusiasm in London in the Year 1702*, written by a most worthy Bishop of London, Edmund Gibson, who was inveighing against the rise of dissenters from the Anglican church. He was, of course, using the word *enthusiasm* (*en-theos*) in its original sense, namely, "to be possessed by a god." The word then was roughly equated with "intoxication" or "possession" by dissident ideas. Truly, to be possessed by a god is a matter of great moment. But the good Bishop was probably inveighing against such subversive elements as Methodists or Quakers, who found their "enthusiasms," or personal revelations, as a confirmation of something real within them. But apparently someone else's "enthusiasm" may prove a threat to the rest of us.*

It is of profound importance, of course, to know the difference between being possessed by a "god" and possessed by a "complex." Many who have fallen in love, or acted violently, learned too late to consider the difference. To be

---

* With the help of a Drew University librarian, we found that the actual, much more mellifluous title was *The Bishop of London's Pastoral Letter to the People of his Diocese; especially those of the two great cities of London and Westminster: by way of Caution against Lukewarmness on one hand, and Enthusiasm on the other* (London, 1739). (This bestseller is, of course, not to be confused with that other perennial favorite, *The Enthusiasm of Methodists and Papists Considered*, by Bishop Lavington, 1820.)

possessed by a complex is to have our ego consciousness owned by a split-off aspect of ourselves. To be possessed by a god, so to speak, is to be summoned to an obedience to something higher. Even then, we have to ask, Which god? What choices? "What circumstances?" In a previous book* I wrote about a young man who felt possessed by Mars, the Latin god of rage, among other things. As metastatic cells raged within him, he raged as well at the prospect of early death. At least he was conscious of what possessed him in those dark hours.

Of any "possession" we have to ask, "What does it ask of me? and "What are the consequences of this imperative?" Just because it is a god who possesses us does not mean its outcome will be benign or salubrious. Do we not have to attend the distinction between what the gods ask of us and what our ethical responsibilities are? After all, great atrocities have been committed in the name of various gods, or maniacal "enthusiasms." Mob psychology is an enthusiasm. Ordinary people placed in extraordinary circumstances have murdered their fellow humans with considerable enthusiasm, whether their cause was religion, or the state, or some vile prejudice handed down by the generations. As Daniel Goldhagen's book *Hitler's Willing Executioners* illustrates, it is not so difficult to coopt willing psyches and mobilize them in service to murderous enthusiasms.

So much for cautionary considerations, but how, one asks, could a love of the art and science of wines be a "higher calling"? How can any "enthusiasm"? Well, for one, we do not

* The discussion of Fritz Zorn's searing memoir, *Mars*, appears in *Why Good People Do Bad Things: Understanding Our Darker Selves*, p. 53.

choose our enthusiasms; they choose us. The difference is huge. We can acquire an enthusiasm, learn it from someone else, of course, be influenced by those around us, but if it does not occasion *resonance* within us, it will be a passing fancy. *Re-sonance* means to "re-sound," to set off echoes within us, to perseverate within, as a tuning fork hums long after it is struck. Whenever we experience resonance, something continues to hum for us. I recall the great sculptor Henry Moore being asked how he was able to sustain his creativity for so many decades and he replied that his passion was so great that he could not chip it all away. And Yeats, to cite another person who remained a creative soul for many decades, a passionate pursuer of his enthusiasms—whether they were political independence for Ireland, art, occult avenues to mystery, or a woman named Maud—wrote in response to a critique of his continuous growth and change:

> My friends who have it I do wrong
> Whenever I remake my song,
> Should know what issue is at stake:
> It is myself that I remake.

His enthusiasms kept him alive and creative up to his deathbed, where he still described himself as "a wild, wicked old man" who prayed, "Grant me an old man's frenzy, / Myself must I remake."

◆ ◆ ◆

Let us also witness the creative process within each of us through the dream that Cynthia, an investment banker, presented very recently, a dream that brings her into the presence of an old friend, Charles, from Cincinnati. Charles appears, dapper, energetic. Cynthia's mother walks on stage; Charles changes to staid clothing, fitting an investment banker's persona. Moreover, the setting appears to be some sort of funeral home. Charles has his new wife present, and Cynthia's mother presents the new wife with a dress, a dress apparently belonging to the decedent. There the dream ends. Who would make this stuff up? Yet there it is: Cynthia's dream, with Cynthia's friend from high school and, sure enough, Cynthia's mother.

Cynthia received this nocturnal visitation as we all do, with confusion, bemusement, wonder, and mild apprehension. Her associations are critical to why her unconscious drew upon these figures to represent some deeper drama underfoot in her contemporary life. Charles, whom she has not seen for many moons, was adventuresome, willing to change careers, explore, take risks. Her mother was highly risk averse. Charles's new wife would seem to be some new relationship to "the feminine," attached to a more vigorous animus, but her mother still stifles this new possibility with the attire of the old and dead.

When we understand that Cynthia is at a critical juncture in her career, in her life, we see how the unconscious seems to be responding. Cynthia wants to make a change, she wants the freedom to re-create herself, as Charles has modeled for her, but when her "mother complex" shows up it seems to shift "Charles" back into a conventional mode, and cloak him with the dress of the dead. Cynthia's mother is in fact long deceased, but the internalization of her values is far from dead. (Death, like divorce, does not end relationships, as many have learned.) The generic form of the "mother complex," as such having little to do with her actual mother, shows up in her need for security, for choosing the safe and conventional, and for sticking with her investment banking career, which she emotionally outgrew long ago. Her mother's lack of sufficient "enthusiasm" reinforced this timorous attitude, but Cynthia is the author of her own biography these days. Every one of us at some level knows what we want to do, need to do, have to do to live our lives.

The dream has pretty well laid out Cynthia's contemporary dilemma before her consciousness. She has already achieved what she, and her mother, wanted for her, but what did her soul* want? It wants what Cynthia admits to herself she wants, a new life, new ventures, the reclamation of pieces of herself left behind. But the "mother complex" stands in the way. Notice the dream is without solution, for the situation is ongoing. Cynthia is now clearer that what stands in her way is not an outer obstacle, but an inner impediment, namely, an archaic message to please her parent, and to avoid risk. Perhaps there were good reasons in the life of her parent to identify with and reiterate those values, but for Cynthia her developmental dilemma is whether she will surrender to the creative desire of her own psyche to end one form of her journey and begin another, or succumb to the admonitions of the past. Tapping into her emergent enthusiasm will reenergize her and confuse all her financial colleagues, who will be puzzled why someone would slay the cash cow she currently milks. But for many, deep inside, they will also envy her for what she has discovered.

---

* Recall that the literal translation of *psyche* from the Greek means "soul."

As we know, life is a series of passages. In every passage there is a death of some sort, the death of naïveté, the death of a dependency, the death of an understanding of self and world. And, after that death, there is often a terrible "in-between," sometimes lasting years. Our ego understandably does not cotton to the idea of anything dying; vested as it is in its own security and maintenance, it will prolong, resist, deny, as long as it can, the dismantling of the old.* The terrible "in-between" is what often brings people into therapy, for they feel very much alone and ineffective in restoring the former sovereignty of the ego.** I have not only gone through this process often myself, but have attended it with analysands hundreds of times. The good news and bad news are both the same: we are asked to *die*. Only through this death can our natural creativity enact its developmental plan. Sounds easy in theory, but not so cheery to go through. Nonetheless, if one can step back and see that this is the nature of nature, that our own psyche is directing these deaths in order to bring us to the next stage, we might, from time to time, facilitate rather than resist the creative process.

Here is another example of the creative process at work. Although there are many other venues for insight, I choose a dream because dreams are so clearly outside the control of our ego. (If you think you are in charge, order up a certain kind of dream tonight, and see if your psyche pays any attention to you whatsoever.) Moreover, do not dismiss the radi-

---

* As Woody Allen once said, he didn't want to become immortal by someone naming a street after him; he wanted to become immortal by not dying.

** This process of death and rebirth are discussed in much greater detail in my *The Middle Passage: From Misery to Meaning at Mid-Life* and *Creating a Life: Finding Your Individual Path*.

cal summons a dream makes upon us simply because it might employ images from the late-night news or what you read in the paper. How easy it is to evade the summons to this radical creative process within us by seeking to explain it away. The psyche is a scavenger and will borrow or steal from your history, or from recent events, and then bring in some impossible, ahistorical situation, mix them all together and say: "So, how do you like them apples?"

Certainly, most modern psychologies shun dream work by labeling such spectral visitants unimportant firings of neurons, or the dumping of day residue. These dismissive attitudes arise from unspoken, unaddressed fears of those who are yet to stand naked in front of the awesome power of their own unconscious. Were they to track those dreams with fidelity over time, they would have to change their lives, and who wants to do that? Even psychologists do not want to change. But, apparently, our psyche does.

Thomas has led a distinguished public life, a life that achieved much service to his community. In the context of analysis Thomas came to realize that he, like Cynthia above, had lived most of his life choices in unconscious servitude to his mother's wishes. I have described his process in my last two books, and our work continues. In the first book, Thomas is back in university sitting for an exam. He recognizes that a stern examiner, with the voice and tone of his mother, is conducting the exam, but he also suddenly realizes that he does not have to take the exam, or meet her expectations, and he gets up and walks out of the classroom. In the second book I described how his psychologically absent father began to make cameo appearances in his dreams, stirring Thomas's deep hunger for the respect, advice, and model of a father. Also in that book I recounted his dream of a man in scuba gear who comes up out of the water and wishes to engage him in animated conversation, dialogue that the dreamer understands will be directive and empowering. Here is a recent installment of the roughly 180 dreams that Thomas has presented over the last three and a half years:

> I sat on a crowded pew in a worship service of some kind. The minister called a young man near the front and asked him to speak to the congregation. The young man acted strange, looking about as though he didn't know where he was. He stood up, stumbled, and then sat down again. The minister persisted, insisting that he say something. The more confused the young man appeared, the more aggressive the clergyman was in his urging. It was apparent the young man was inebriated or ill.
>
> My father looked at me and said quietly, "Help him."
>
> I got up and took the youth by the arm and outside to my car. I drove him out of the city into the countryside. Soon we came to a cabin in the woods, where we waited for my father.
>
> I went to the bathroom. When I returned the young man seemed fine. He was at the stove frying bacon. The aroma filled the cabin and smelled delicious.

Again, who among us thinks such stuff up? Thomas immediately identified with the young man who was confused and disabled. His recollection of the religious practices of his youth were that they were coercive and synonymous with his mother's values and intentions for him, which he, like most children, internalized and lived out as best he could.

By now in the analytic process, however, we see that his father is much more present, providing the sort of advice and energy that so counterbalances the childhood domination of his mother. He takes the young man, his inner life left behind, from the ego structures of the church and city to the restorative unconscious where that undernourished part of himself revives. Thomas recalls the delight he took from his favorite food, bacon, as a youth, and he is heartened here by the clear feeling that father energy is finally on its way to further the healing of this young man. So our growth and healing never ends, nor does the summons to be more attentive to such an agenda.

Another, even more recent, dream adds to this unfolding, healing story. Thomas dreams:

> I am walking in a large yard. My dad comes out dressed in a beautiful new suit and topcoat—gray with herringbone pattern. I notice he was wearing new shoes, tie, and white shirt.
>
> He was preparing to leave for Great Britain. I touched him on the shoulder and told him how good I thought he looked. He was touched by my compliment. We walked a short distance together and I noticed he was several inches taller than me.

We see how these images, which arise from the telluric depths of the psyche, demonstrate that the healing process continues. His once-missing father now turns up, looking rather spiffy, as the carrier of a more generative energy. The dreamer's association with Great Britain was with the exciting idea of travel, foreign adventure, and something "great."

At dream's end, the two, father and son, are clearly in a more harmonious relationship, suggesting how the "missing father" complex, and the compensatory empowerment it embodies, has evolved, bringing Thomas greater access to the captaincy of his own journey.

And now, months later, just before I sent this manuscript off to the publisher, Thomas brought me still one more dream, the short version of which is that he is emerging from a dark, decrepit structure. Across the street is a blazing, luminous pharmacy labeled THE SOJOURNER TRUTH PHARMACY! From this place his father steps forth, again nattily dressed. Thomas is proud to be his son, and they walk off down the street arm in arm. Once again, that emerging father energy, so missing in his childhood, steps forth in a healing, empowering way, and the solitary traveler that Thomas feels he has often been is now on the Dharma Road, the sacred sojourn, the path of Truth, after all.

What these dreams have brought Thomas is a linkage to his early enthusiasm for life, a powerful life force that was mostly quashed and channeled by someone else's agenda. His enthusiasm for his unfolding journey has in turn led to the recovery of interests, talents, and investigations that fired the imagination of his youth. When we are doing what is right for us, the psyche provides enthusiasm—that is, the energy to support our investment in life.

If we should ever doubt that our essential nature is creative, we need only turn to our dreams as one illustration. As a folk proverb has it, we should take our dreams seriously because we are not intelligent enough to create them. Yet they are *our* dreams, phenomena rising from the self-regulatory psyche. Just how is it that such a synthetic, synoptic intelligence abides within all of us? Those "scientists" who debunk dreams have not really spent any effort over time to track their motifs, correctives, insights, and intimations. So you, the reader, will dream tonight, and just what is your third-grade teacher doing in your place of current business? Could it be that what is most troubling you today is an issue that has its genesis way back then, and is personified in her guest appearance on your inner stage? Could it be that this spontaneously generative set of images can open you further to the essential mystery that courses through all of us?

This creative process is found in all of us, and also asks much of us. It comes to us as symptoms that embody hidden correctives, compensatory dreams, depressions that tell us that psyche will no longer cooperate with our faulty choices, and so on. This creative process always asks a death of some old attitude, which is why we resist our own growth and development so often that something else has to take over, or our children have to carry out the unfinished projects for us. What we may also not have considered along the way is that every time we have shunned our summons to creativity, left undeveloped a talent or capacity, we have thereby removed that gift from the world. Our gift to the world is honored by bringing our best self to it; paradoxically, we do that by sacrificing ego comforts to our creative process, which, killing off the old, drives the project that we are forward.

FOOLISH PASSIONS

As for those "foolish" passions, let us remember two things. They may only be foolish to the world, but they are not foolish to our souls, or they would not have the power to attract libido, mobilize and guide its vectors. There is a big difference between wasting time—our popular culture offers a vast arena of possibilities for doing so—and having a passion. Jung noted that without some quickening of the spirit, we would all indulge our greatest occupation—idleness. But a quickened spirit summons us out of the sibilant susurrus of sleep into the world of passion. Remember that the word *passio* is the Latin word for "suffering." A passion is something we feel so deeply, so intensely that it hurts, yet much of worth comes from such a hurt. All of us have passions, but because they, too, ask much of us, we often dissemble, slip-slide away, and leave them along the road behind us.* Most of us have left passions behind, but if we are blessed by fate to live long enough, we have the opportunity to revive some of them, if not literally, then to at least symbolically value what aspect of our lives they represent.

Some years ago my wife and I visited the Museum of American Art, which is a part of the Smithsonian National Museum of American Art in Washington, DC. There we came across a large, bizarre, but compelling work of "folk art" with the unwieldy title: *The Throne of the Third Heaven of the Nations Millennium General Assembly*. It seems that this work was found in the garage of a District janitor, James Hampton (1909–64), who worked for the federal government's General Services Administration, and who had through his long years of laboring gathered discarded tinfoil,

---

* More than one person has said to me, "Writing must be easy for you." I do not know why they would say that. It is a personal suffering that demands that I work an hour here and there at the end of a long workday, sacrifice a normal life, and yet continue to show up in a disciplined way. But this passion rewards me with those occasional moments when the right word falls into place, from somewhere. These are just brief moments, always paid for, but worth it.

mostly from chewing gum, and many other "found objects." Over the years he labored by day through heat and cold and gloom of night to discharge his civic duty, but by night he indulged his passion. He brought those many pieces of foil home and assembled a large work, a visionary work of what Heaven might look like. His work is wondrously baroque, coming from a "simple" man, and is a profound gift to all of us. It consists of approximately 180 pieces that meld together old furniture, jelly jars, carpet cylinders, and much, much more with glue, tape, and pins. We cannot help but scratch our heads, and stand in wonder, at his foolish passion. This man may or may not have found Heaven after he died—which is when this work was finally discovered by others—but he certainly shares space with what Hart Crane called "the visionary company," namely, those who pierce the diaphanous membrane between this tangible, frangible world, and the other, perduring world that lies on the slope side of conventional reality. I was moved by his foolish passion, touched by his devotion, and reminded that each of us is obliged to construct our own myth, for—as that earlier visionary William Blake said—if we do not create our own myth, we will be enslaved to someone else's.

This evening, while out walking after supper, I came across a woman with a small white dog. We have walked together more than once and I always carry dog crunchies for such encounters. She said, in the midst of a conversation about her dog's health, "No one would understand why I care about her so much." I said that I could and did. In fact, my heart leaps up every time I see that small white dog because he reminds me of Shadrach, our Lhasa apso, who died in 2000. We still grieve him, speak of him as though he were alive, and every day, en route to work, at a certain curve in the road where the skyline of downtown Houston hoves into view, I tell him how much we love him. In fact, I am half persuaded that one of these days a gaggle of saffron-robed monks from Tibet will show up to announce his reincarnation as the next Dalai Lama, or some such exalted office. Whatever high office he may then attain will pale before his privileged place in our hearts. So I think I do know something of what this lady feels for her foolish passion.

Those who know me know me as a worker, some would say a compulsive worker. One of my compensatory passions is reading; it is not an escape, for reading usually takes me deeper into something that then asks a response from me. Another is sports. As a child, I lived for reading and sports. The former has been a constant, the latter something I am now returning to as my timbers begin to creak and groan.

Let me give an example of how such foolish passion shows up in my current thinking by this memoir on, of all things, baseball. Let me take you, then, out to the old ball game. "Game" it is, but lest you think it is only a game, remember what surrealist Paul Eluard once said: "There *is* another world, and it is this one." So if the reader does not like sports, per se, read on, please, for this is really not about sports at all.

THE GREEN FIELDS OF MEMORY

"President Roosevelt died," my father said in April of 1945. I knew this was important because the radio played classical music for three days. I had never heard classical music before. Days later, my father said, "Hitler just died." "Does this mean we can go home?" I asked. "Yes, soon." (Because of the war, we were in Racine, Wisconsin, rather than my home town of Springfield, Illinois.) That was more than six decades ago, yet they are very clear memories. Three years after that, my father said, "Babe Ruth died today." "Who is that?" I asked. "The greatest baseball player who ever lived," he said. He had moisture in his eyes this time, so this ratiocinative eight-year-old surmised that Babe Ruth was apparently more important than Roosevelt and Hitler. Shortly after that I asked for and received my first baseball accoutrement. It was one of those flat leather gloves only a bit bigger than the size of one's hand, with a bit of leather strung between the thumb and first finger. From that moment, and for years to come, I lived to play baseball.

Everyone I knew in our neighborhood in Springfield rooted for the Cardinals, and if not them, the Cubbies. I never met a White Sox fan, though the distance from Springfield to Comiskey Park was no farther than that to Wrigley Field. Yet, perversely, I became, and am now embarrassed to admit, a Yankee fan, for in that era no one had heard of somebody named George Steinbrenner. But I loved their quaint NY logo, had seen Gary Cooper in *The Pride of the Yankees*, and together they were enough to make me a true believer in America, the unshakable probity of certain heroes, and the pinstripes of the Bronx Bombers. When Gehrig said that he was "the luckiest man on Earth," I believed him, or at least until later when I saw patients choking to death from amyotrophic lateral sclerosis. For years I won dimes betting my friend Kent, who perversely followed the Dodgers, perhaps because they had the great Jackie Robinson, while I celebrated how DiMaggio and Mantle carried on the Ruth and Gehrig legacy. I never got to see a real Yankee game until many years later, but I was exhilarated when I was able to buy a ragged Yankee cap with the NY logo with my lawn-mowing money from another kid down on his luck. No purchase in my life has ever brought such satisfaction as that ragged cap. The Yankee logo was, literally, sacred to me, and the reticulated towers of Yankee Stadium radiated as the terminus of a grail quest that I knew I would have to undertake when I grew up.

Now, these six decades later, I take a special satisfaction when "The Boss," and the best team money can buy, lose. What happened, why does it matter at all, and why does this silly game still have a hold on my soul? And why, like Hearst's "Rosebud" sled in *Citizen Kane*, does that cap, with its magical logo, still mean so much, when its facsimile is so easily available today in any store or via the Internet? Yet, even more, why I would not dream of wearing one today?

◆ ◆ ◆

Garry Wills once pointed out that the etymology of *paradise* suggested an enclosed green space. No matter how many games we may attend, who can deny that rush, that archetypal intimation of coming home, perhaps stealing home to the Edenic place, when one walks up through the concrete corridors and that lush green field first comes into view? (As a therapist, I have learned not to blink or gasp when the most horrific events are related to me, but when that rich green field comes into view, I always remember Dylan Thomas's "Fern Hill." His memory of his aunt's paradisiacal apple farm in Wales abides with him through darker, more distant

days, contending with his adult awareness that "time allows /
in all his tuneful turning so few and such morning songs /
before the children green and golden / follow him out of
grace.")

So how, and why, does baseball still have a hold on me,
and why does this foolish passion persist? Baseball is one of
the few *constants* in an evanescent world. If we could trans-
port one of the nineteenth-century New York Knickerbock-
ers onto the field today, he would have no doubt how to play
the game. Hit the ball, run to first, slide into third ahead of
the ball. This is as clear as the expectations of a mariner on the
Aegean millennia ago: sail the boat, seize the prize, don't
drown, bring the damn thing home.

Another appeal of baseball, this foolish passion, is its
clarity. There are winners and losers, even though most of us
know by now that in real life we are all losers, that you never
get ahead of the game, that in the end the game gets
you—whatever game you are playing, whatever game is playing you. Moreover, the statistics of baseball make it relatively
possible to hold the contemporary up against the classic,
even if we debate the differences between the dead ball and
the juiced ball, between the beer once scarfed down in the
seventh-inning stretch by Ruth and Cobb with today's juiced,
jaded, and roided-up millionaires. What was Johnson's ERA,
and how does that compare with Koufax? How would Campy
do against Dickey and Bench and Berra? The stats are there,
seducing us to forget Disraeli's observation that there are
"three kinds of lies: lies, damned lies, and statistics."

In a world grown dirty gray, there is also something
clean about baseball. The ball is hit, fair or foul, with longitudes and latitudes to tell us which. Not since the death of

Dante in 1321, when the Western world still had relative consensus on the longitudes and latitudes of the soul, can we know fair from foul with any certainty. After all, in our time, did not Yeats's "Crazy Jane" tell us "fair and foul are next of kin." After Samuel Beckett and *Godot*, no white stripes remain on the field to tell us right from wrong, or where we are really headed.

Baseball, thus, is much about *nostalgia*, a word whose Greek origins speak of our "painful longing for home." We are exiles in our time, *entre deux guerres,* as Eliot put it, lost generations, Stein added, including the Boomers who boom a lot to hide their systemic desuetude and drift toward irrelevance. Only baseball offers clarity, for the moment, when nothing else does. When I saw *The Pride of the Yankees,* I could still believe we faithfully observed the Constitution of the United States, could count on the probity of the president, and trust the purity of American intentions. Today, only baseball remains. Between the white lines only does a predictable, albeit provisional, clarity preside. The short hop, the cutoff man missed, the slider that hits the corner . . . minor irritations in a minutely calibrated universe.

When I began to teach my son to play baseball, I carefully explained to him where the bases were, and the sequence in which one made their acquaintance. He promptly ran from home to second. "No, you go to first, first," I said. "Dad," this ten-year-old said, "first base is only arbitrary. I can go to second first." He was metaphors ahead of me already. He was already—without having read Jacques Derrida—a post-modern deconstructionist, and I was merely modern. So much for clarity of field, fixity of construct, and post-modern transfers of signification.

Yet so much of even baseball has changed. The players change cities with each contract. No longer can one consider that Pepper Martin will be a Cardinal, Whitey Ford a Yankee, or Duke Snider a Dodger. It is much more an assemblage of mercenaries now. Of course it always was, but one gets the sense that in the old days, most of the mercenaries played because they really loved it and considered themselves privileged to get paid for doing what they loved to do anyway. Number 4, that Gehrig guy, was accosted on a road trip in the lobby of a hotel by a little old lady who asked him what he and the big guys around him did for a living. "We play baseball, ma'am," he said. "Why don't you get a job?" she said. They were boys in men's bodies, doing what we all want to do, continue the games that boys play. The *puer aeternus* today is a pathogenic complex describing a boy who never grows up, who may float from woman to woman, and who never works anything through—a playboy; but that youthful sense of play persists in healthy form; the summons of the game for the sake of the game is still a value timeless in our souls, floating as we do on the green fields of memory and aspiration. It was no good for the "Iron Horse," who played 2,130 consecutive games, to explain to the lady that it was a job also,* that they used equine liniment to nurse those aching bodies back onto the field, for she was really onto them—they *were* boys then, not mercenaries with negotiators and agents in their posse. When one loses the boy, something dies forever.

---

* While huge sacrifices were the norm throughout all strata of society during World War II, President Roosevelt insisted that professional baseball continue, knowing that it was something more than a diversion, that it sustained a community connection whose balm was good for the soul.

Finally, I got to see the Cards play the Giants at Sportsman's Park in St. Loo. Stan the Man was there with his corkscrew stance, freckled Red Schoendienst, Enos "Country" Slaughter, and Harry Caray's voice on the PA—what wonders they were! But the man I wanted to see was number 24, the "Say Hey Kid." Paul Geil was pitching. Willie swung mightily at a high heater, whirled around in centrifugal fury, and fell to earth with the force of his spent swing. He got up laughing and dusted himself off . . . laughing. Everyone laughed with him, everyone, especially the Cardinal fans. We all knew Willie Mays was a kid, like us, doing the thing he loved. Who could not love him for his joy?

Still another deep level in which baseball functions for us all, and still does today, is that it provides a way *for men to talk to each other*. We are pathologically isolated from women, even more from each other, and even more still from ourselves. So, we need a bridge to help us over the abyss. Politics and religion used to work, but in red and blue states today they only divide. But "What do you think the Mets are going to do this year?" and "Did you see Rivera shut down the Sox the other night?" still works. Moreover, it is still a way in which dads have something to transmit to their sons, quite apart from relaying the dreary prospect of being an economic beast of burden. Never mind that there is no tribal lore to transmit, never mind that we have so little else in common; this foolish passion baseball provides a meeting ground, a momentary bridge.

◆ ◆ ◆

I usually played second or shortstop. One night our third baseman was sick and I was shifted there. On an obvious bunt situation, already pulled in tight, I rushed home. The batter squared around and smacked the ball, which caromed off my cheek toward the opponent's bench. I was knocked a bit loopy, for as I went after the ball, I was convinced that I was underwater and was trying to swim between the reedy legs of their third base coach to get to the ball. As reported to me, some yahoo in the crowed yelled, with guffaw and crowd approval, "Hey, kid, you catch the ball with your glove, not your face." He was sitting next to my father, who, a gentle, peaceful man, had some words with him. I learned all this later, and was proud of my father for standing up for me. I wish I had sometimes stood up as well for him as he did for me that night.

Through the power of this foolish passion to form common ground momentarily between men, we can use shorthand like, "Texas leaguer," "can of corn," "suicide squeeze," "split-finger fastball," and other forms of mythopoeic arcana that serve to link those otherwise separated from each other and themselves. The celebration of rituals so common to the game, the lingua franca of the trade, the deontological clarity of fair and foul, the affective surge that accompanies the bottom of the ninth, provide religious dimensions to our fragmented experience. This is why such foolish passions endure. It is a silly waste of energy to the uninitiated, only one grade above smacking a white ball around a green sward, but to those who have tasted the dust, smelled the oil rubbed into a new glove, or felt the thwack of the bat ripple through their entire body, it is a religion of sorts, a religion that links one to the tribal fathers, to the timeless, to a presumptive fixity of fair and foul, and therefore not to be casually discounted in this time or the next.

With this foolish passion, there is something tangible to learn, and it is learnable. Most of our pursuits, especially in the "virtual realities" we inhabit, are exhaustingly elusive. As a therapist, I know that I am always dealing with the invisible world, though it is a world at least as real as the world we see. (Indeed, it creates the world we see.) But baseball offers a world we can see, and asks for skills that most of us were willing to learn, a discipline to which most of us were willing to submit: how to judge while the ball is still in transit from the rubber to home, and the batter beginning the first phase of the swing, where the ball, if hit, is likely to land; how to slide while wearing spikes for the first time without breaking an ankle, as the Giants' Monte Irvin did; or how to slide away from the throw to provide as little target for the tag as possible; or how to lead off just enough to rattle the pitcher in his stretch, without suffering the humiliation of getting picked off, or falling for the oldest of dumbbell plays, the hidden-ball trick. These things clamored for learning, and we learned them, and felt that we had, in this narrow frame at least, learned something, and even occasionally mastered something. Something learned, really learned. After Husserl and phenomenology, after Heidegger and *Daseinanalysis*, after Wittgenstein and "language games," something learned, finally. So: "Find the relay man; hold your position but lean toward the gap, shorten your grip on the bat so slightly that they don't know you intend to bunt." Something learned— never again so much learned, so clearly. Never again, ever. How grateful one remains for that. Never discount that grateful feeling.

◆ ◆ ◆

Like many boys, I wanted to wear those Gotham pinstripes. Ruth (#3) and Gehrig (#4) were gone, as was DiMaggio (#5), their heir, but by the time I was an adolescent, it was a kid from Spavinaw, Oklahoma (#7). If someone from Spavinaw could make the bigs, then surely I could. Later I would learn that this is the fallacy of false analogy. It seems that the gods gave the almost perfect body to Mickey Mantle, not *moi*.

For a few, brief, adolescent moments, when I learned I did not have the talent, that I had to quit baseball forever and go to work at age sixteen to help the family, I felt that I had invented tragedy.* Decades later—though he once owned a Holiday Inn of his own in Joplin, Missouri, where he briefly played on the way up to Yankee Stadium; though he batted .353, hit 52 dingers, and had 130 ribbies in 1965 (those stats are burned in my mind); though he could fly to haul down line-drive gappers; though he got a liver transplant in Dallas—I came to learn that real tragedy was not my shortfall from the baseball gods, but really being Mickey Mantle.

Though I had a bone disease of my own, Mickey's osteomyelitis was positively heroic. The photo of him bandaged, leaking blood at Yankee Stadium, was more heroic than *Sands of Iwo Jima*. I was not then informed about the booze, the women, his devouring anxiety about playing in the bigs. I presumed that not being Mickey Mantle was sad; later I learned that being Mickey Mantle was sad, sometimes really sad.

---

* I was not the only person invested in this fantasy. A grade-school friend of mine recently reminisced that he fully believed that I would in fact become a Major League player. He did not add that he was disappointed in me too.

Tragedy is such a devalued concept in our time. Actually, it is a heroic sensibility, a summons to consciousness, an admonition to greater reverence for the gods. We are raised up, serve as playthings to the gods, fall, and then the responsibility for such a tumble is ours, we are told. Wait a moment—how is that *our* fault, we who so casually confuse "fate" with "destiny"? Fate is what is given to us; destiny is what we are summoned to become. In the interplay of the two, human character plays a role. *Hubris*, or the fantasy that we know enough to know enough, seduces us toward choices that lead to unintended consequences. *Hamartia*, the failure to see clearly enough, to see humbly enough, is a lens through which we imperfectly envision the world, unavoidably distorting and reductive, but convincing at the moment nonetheless.

So Mickey was born with a genetic heritage, a disorder that took his ancestors early, and yet he wore a beautiful, godlike body—an Adonis who could run from a dead start to first in 3.1 seconds. His genetically doomed father, perhaps compensating for his own unlived life (Jung said that "the greatest burden the child must bear is the unlived life of the parent"), taught Mickey to bat both ways. Such an unnatural act reduces the advantage that right- or left-handed pitchers can achieve, and ought to be worth ten points in the batting average—that absolute, eschatological moral index—by the end of the year. And so it was with blinding speed, great hand-eye coordination, and the pinstripes, those glorious pinstripes, that he stepped into the circle of divinity.

On another occasion my parents took me to Sportsman's Park to see the sad-sack Brownies against the Yanks. It was a sacred pilgrimage to me. Mickey went hitless that day, but during batting practice he lifted one up and out of the field into the third tier. That swing confirmed that he was for real—a god, indeed.

But Mickey lived beyond those years of walking among the gods. (Where have you gone, Joe DiMaggio, and Marilyn, and Elvis?) He lived hard, and he lived rough. He said it was because he did not realistically expect, given his genetic heritage, to live very long. Like the jazz man Hubie Blake, who, at age ninety-nine, said, "I would have treated myself better if I had known I would live this long," Mickey pushed and abused his body.

Perhaps he had to do so in order to fulfill the tragic cycle: a man raised to greatness, cursed/blessed by the gods, brought to acts of high moment, and then hurtled to humbling defeat. However, in the tragic vision, the whole point is to bring one back into right relationship with the gods. Lear, not a bad man, but a foolish man, does not understand what love is, until the gods stipple knowledge on his aging brow. He learns what love is, what abides, and is the better for it. Did Mickey complete the tragic cycle? I do not know. I do know that he repented some of his decisions, and their impact on his family.

Aristotle said that the citizens of Athens who watched the tragic trilogies experienced the catharsis of two profound emotions: pity and fear. Pity: "I experience, and grieve, the suffering of another."

Fear: "I fear that I, too, will fall into some similar pit that perhaps lies beneath my nervous tread." The philosopher believed that these affectively evocative enactments on stage actually served a therapeutic, healing function for the public. They could look on in horror at what happens when we meet the gods, be chastened to greater mindfulness around their own precarious steps, and experience the release of emotions that, unexpressed, might prove toxic. I still revere the Mick—the subway series with the Bums, the fleet antelope running down a fly to right center, the Ballantine Blasts—but I would not want to be Mickey. The gods sent him, and *moi*, to our separate tragic engagements. But I only got a clue as to how tough it must have been to be Mickey after I got a clue as to how tough it was proving to be myself. Unlike Mickey, I am still here for now, kicking it around, still working on figuring it out.

◆ ◆ ◆

Goethe's personal motto was *Dauer im Wechseln*—"what abides amid change." So, what provides continuity amid our sundry discontinuities? Certainly the Self abides our constant deaths. Our cells divide, die, generate at a slowing pace, and we are not the same bodies now as the moment before. Memory helps, but we cannot even answer the simple question "Of what are we unconscious?" Yet there are, from time to time, points of reference, benchmarks, lines drawn from which we get a provisional baseline, a fleeting summons to the next goal, a moment's thought that this absurd, arbitrary game we call our lives might actually mean something. Sometimes a foolish passion opens a slit into the mystery. And, as Louis Armstrong said of jazz, those who have to have it explained to them will never know.

◆ ◆ ◆

Things fall apart . . . the center cannot hold, as Yeats proclaimed in 1917. And since that slippage began, most things we cherish have gone still farther south, fast. Yet certain moments abide, certain foolish passions continue to nourish and animate. Perhaps, even at this moment, it still is the bottom of the ninth, runners on second and third, 2 and 0 on the batter, and the pitch is loosed. . . . All is open, it seems, *still*; the game is on, *now*; the game is on, and *we are in it*.

Chapter Nine

THAT WE ENGAGE SPIRITUAL CRISES, AND OTHER BAD DAYS AT THE OFFICE

*S*ome years back a man grew up in special circumstances. Perhaps superstitiously, perhaps sagely, his parents had reason to believe that their child would somehow grow up to harm them, so they hired someone to kill him. The assassin hired, looking at the helpless baby, took pity on him and left him by the roadside. Another goodhearted person picked him up, raised him, and in time this child grew into an adult, traveled to another land, and in a fit of road rage slew a man at a crossroads. When he visited the next city, he met a widow to whom he was strangely attracted, and she to him, and they married; and soon, being the smartest guy on the block, he came to hold high office in that city. Then things went downhill, really downhill, and he subsequently learned that the man he had murdered was his father, and the woman he married was his mother . . . and you think you had a bad day at the office!

So, this man had to spend the rest of his life trying to figure out how it all went so wrong, to understand how his intelligence failed the simplest, most important of matters: his identity, his flawed discernment of the inscrutable will of the gods who set him forth into such circumstances, and yet his humbling confession that the choices made were his alone. ("Apollo set this fate upon me, but the hand that wounded me was mine own.") So this man Oedipus, reputedly the wisest man in Thebes, came to the worst of spiritual crises, yet persisted in humble learning, and at the end of his life received the blessing of those condign gods. While we stand in horror at his deeds, we honor him for his sincere desire to come through, to perdure, and arrive at last at wisdom.

Might that we do as much in our journeys.

◆ ◆ ◆

Spiritual crises happen to us every day. Most of them are sufficiently low grade, devoid of enduring consequences, so we pay no attention and keep on rolling. *A spiritual crisis occurs when our identity, our roles, our values, or our road map are substantially called into question, prove ineffective, or are overwhelmed by experience that cannot be contained by our understandings of self and world.* Recently I spoke with a man whose life is full of business, socializing, and tons of public recognition for his successes. Yet he is tired, anxious, and depressive, without being depressed. For years he has been staying ahead of "the game." As that great American philosopher-psychologist Satchel Paige once said, "Don't look back—something might be gaining on you." Something is always gaining on us—if not consequences for decisions made and consciousness avoided, then age itself, mortality—rapping on our floorboards, seeking entrance through the cracks in our cover story. This good man, like the rest of us, assembled a false self to manage anxiety and meet the world in constructive terms, but he has been sitting on a ton of unprocessed grief from the past—a missing mother, a disconnected father, and a world of expectations that he "make something of himself" to compensate for their shame and sorrow. Like most of us, this man has struggled mightily within the premises of this adaptive personality, and has achieved much of worth, and yet he is tired, spent, and wanting surcease from the burdensome assignment. While he came to discuss some business distresses, what he is circling is a spiritual crisis, a summons to reconfigure his entire life.

Spiritual crises come to us for several reasons. Among them are: 1) trauma—personal or cultural; 2) autogenous swampland visitations; 3) discrepancies between expectations and outcomes; 4) incongruence between map and terrain; and 5) a dystonic relationship between false and natural self.

TRAUMA–PERSONAL OR CULTURAL

Life hurts, and sometimes it hurts a great deal. We are extraordinarily flexible, possess genetic programming to survive, even prevail, and we gain resilience as we age, and yet we still hurt easily. Trauma occurs when our defenses and presumptions, whether somatic, emotional, or intellectual, are overrun. We feel powerless and at the mercy of life. This crisis is in fact our common condition, for each of us has gotten the same message identified earlier in this book: "The world is big, and you are not; the world is powerful, and you are not. Now, figure out a way to survive, managing that!"

Our trauma may be cultural or personal. In the fourth

century of the Common Era, St. Augustine felt obliged to write both a treatise against suicide and *City of God*. With the collapse of the Roman Empire, the spread of "barbarism," and the collapse of institutional certainties, many early Christians, believing that another, better world awaited them, sought to take their lives and get there sooner. In *City of God*, Augustine offered a comparison between a transient human world and an enduring divine order. Believing in the latter, he argued, might help one survive the distresses of the former. We live in a similarly shattered Weltanschauung where cultural distractions urgently seek to mask the demise of tribal mythologies, where sex, power, money are offered up as "connections" to replace the linking to the transcendent mythic images once granted. Anyone with a modicum of consciousness is traumatized by this current world, with its move from instinctual guidance, sympathetic resonance with natural rhythms of seasons and death and rebirth, to "virtual" realities such as economics, data processing, and daily distractions no more evolved than the bread and circuses* through which the Roman emperors distracted their citizenry from their august, megalomaniacal depredations. (Today, there is no more efficacious diversion than the mantra *terrorism* to divert one from the plumb line of the soul.) In this setting, as Augustine intuited, one has to find an order of one's own, an order persisting amid the distractions and disorders of one's time. Some still look "upward" to find this transcendent order, and some find it there; some, by looking "upward," merely avoid taking on the task of find-

---

* *Panem et circum*, bread and circuses, materialism and distraction—sound familiar?

ing meaning for themselves; and some now look "inward" to find this centering order. Of this latter group, Albert Camus's paradox is especially applicable. He said that life is meaningful precisely because it is absurd. What I believe he means is that if it is "meaningful," then it is someone else's understanding, a received package, and may or may not be consonant with one's own journey. By considering life absurd, we are obliged to make choices, real choices with real consequences, and thereby are the active agents in creating and affirming our value system. The more consonant these value elections are with our inner lives, our souls, the more meaningfully we will experience these choices, and the more we will feel supported from within.

SWAMPLANDS OF THE SOUL

Elsewhere I have written at great length* on the subject of how, sooner or later, all of us are ushered by fate, by the actions of others, by choices we make, both conscious and unconscious, into places we do not wish to visit. Such rooms in our common psychic mansion we label depression, loss, grief, addiction, anxiety, envy, shame, and the like. Such is our humanity. In these dismal environs we are flooded by anxiety because the fact of being out of control is no longer deniable. Accordingly, and typically, we tend to kick into our former management systems—denial, projection onto others, addiction, frenetic activity—and we mire deeper and deeper in the swamp. In those moments we suffer a spiritual crisis because we have no place to go, or rather, no means by

* See bibliography for *Swamplands of the Soul: New Life from Dismal Places.*

which to go there, and we suffer our powerlessness and the failure of our provisional management systems.

While we cannot avoid these swamplands, each of them is a critical junction whereby we must make choices that prove either psychologically enlarging or diminishing. In moments of powerlessness, we may paradoxically find a terrible freedom, and thereby wrest our spirits away from delimiting *Ananke*, or necessity. Even Oedipus—no Pollyanna he—was able to say, "I look about myself and all is in ruin, and I say life is good."

DISCREPANCY BETWEEN EXPECTATIONS AND OUTCOMES

All of us have expectations, and necessarily so. We also have projections, drives, and programs that leave us and enter the world in search of places upon which to invest their agenda. Thus, we look, for example, to "romance" to fulfill us. We find "the magical other,"* the one upon whom our projection falls, and we surrender to the fantasy of homecoming through the beloved. Yet as we all know, behind that mysterious "other" lies a humble reality: ordinary people like us, with both riches and limitations, and with agendas of their own to be projected onto us.

Similarly, we project our deepest hopes, needs, fears onto institutions, ideologies, governments, places of employment, and the gods. We expect our company, our school, our church to love us and take care of us; we expect our partner

---

* Please see *The Eden Project: In Search of the Magical Other* for a fuller discussion of romance, love, and the psychodynamics of relationship, whether the "magical other" is the beloved, an institution, an ideology, or God.

to meet our needs as our parents perhaps failed to do; we expect amorphous divinities to make it all right in the end. What is famously called "the midlife crisis" is precisely such an erosion of programs and projections.* We expect that by investing sincere energy in a career, a relationship, a set of roles, that they will return the investment in manifold, satisfying ways. We feverishly renew the projections, up the ante, and anxiously repress the insurgence of doubt once more.

We do not realize that a projection has occurred, for it is an unconscious mechanism of our energic unconscious. Only after it has painfully dissolved may we begin to recognize that we placed such a large agenda on such a frangible place, that we asked too much of the beloved, of others, of institutions, perhaps of life itself.

INCONGRUENCE BETWEEN MAP AND TERRAIN

We all receive maps: this is what life is about—do this, do that, don't do this or that; value this, pursue that; count on this; avoid that, and so on. Received maps come from parents, religious and educational sources, popular culture, and from history. Sometimes these maps are helpful and rewarding, and sometimes they are not. Sometimes we begin to cotton to the fact that we are living someone else's map, someone else's complexes, or someone else's individuation task. In the medieval Grail story the text tells us that in his pursuit of the sacred, each knight went to a place in the

---

* This midlife encounter is discussed in greater detail in *The Middle Passage* and *Finding Meaning in the Second Half of Life*.

forest where there was no path, for it would prove a shameful thing to take the path that someone else had trod before. As early as the twelfth century of the common era we see undeniable evidence that someone recognized that there is a path meant for each of us, and that we may have been spending time heretofore on someone else's path.

Nonetheless, for the first half of life, we all take someone else's path, someone else's map of the terrain, and understandably so. Who else were we to count on? Who, after all, ever told us that we were here to live a wholly personal journey, with features unique to us alone, and that our surest guide obliged we pay attention to our instincts and intuition, track our dreams, and trust our soul to offer us both correctives and intimations on our paths?

We may learn much from others, from history, and from our tribe, but we also have to work things through ourselves. One of the classic examples of this experience of discrepancy is the map that our brother Job received from his tribe, the one that advised that right actions lead to right consequences, and that he could trust that a quid pro quo exists between his believing tribe and the gods. Among other things, the book of Job is the account of the profound disillusionment of a good man who is dismayed, confused, and thrown into the deepest crisis when his understanding, his projections are not sustained by the universe into which he was thrown. That he comes out of this a "religious" man, as opposed to a "pious good boy," is testimony to the power of his disillusionment, and the strength of character that he finds to move through the discrepancy between map and terrain to a reconfigured terrain, a revised understanding. He is much less comfortable at story's end, but he is a larger soul, and in a larger relationship with the mystery of life, which he once so casually took for granted.

DYSTONIC RELATIONS BETWEEN THE FALSE AND THE NATURAL SELF

The bad news is that our psyche frequently beats up on us. The good news is that our psyche frequently beats up on us. In our infantilized time, suffering seems an affront, as though we are to have it all figured out, have management systems in place, or have medications to remove it from us. From the superficial standpoint so popular in our healing armamentaria, symptoms are to be removed as quickly as possible. We employ vast engines of ingenuity devoted to this task. However, from the psychodynamic perspective, we consider symptoms messages, expressions of psyche's dismay at our lives, our choices, our values. This dismay comes to us via disturbances in the body, in troubling emotional discord, in our dreams, in our relationships, and in our history. Reading these symptoms as invitations to reconsider our relationship to the Self, revise our values and plans, and renew our relationship to mystery as it moves through the world and through us, is a most challenging task. But it is the means by which we recover a relationship to the gods, to the essential mystery that lies within our individual psyches just as it courses through history.

Symptoms invite us to reconsider our maps, revisit the terrain, revision our journeys, and reconsider our purposes. Finding that the map we have been using is no longer adequate is always disconcerting, even anxiety provoking, but it is the beginning of a process by which we come to a better map, a more interesting terrain, a more considered life. The astonishing fact is that when we suffer from inner, as opposed to outer, sources, our psyche is registering a huge fact, a life-transforming fact, if we can surrender to it, namely: The psyche has a better plan for our lives than our ego's plan, or our culture's plan. This sounds simple enough, even reasonable, but no ego consciousness is thrilled about overthrow, critique, or humbling. Yet from this bewildering deconstruction, the real project our lives embody can emerge, and be rendered palpable, which always requires of us, despite our desires for comfort and predictability, a change and enlargement of consciousness.

◆ ◆ ◆

Perhaps we've all experienced these five categories of discrepancy, and suffered the gap between the ego's fantasy of sovereignty and the reality of the soul. What, then, is our arsenal of options for dealing with these crises? They are 1) collapse of some kind; 2) regression; 3) distraction; 4) narcotization; or 5) transformation.

COLLAPSE

When our ego plan, our world view, our presumptions, our maps fail to adequately manage anxiety and move our life forward in search of the satisfaction of our needs, we sometimes experience collapse. When a culture loses its myth, it usually folds quickly. Just consider the collapse of Polynesian civilization a single generation after the missionaries and merchants arrived. These invading hoards were not importing a higher truth; they were importing ideas, practices, and tools that imposed larger questions on indigenous populations than their mythic resources could address. Indigenous American civilizations similarly collapsed, although it usually took more than one generation. In the case of the Kiowa, whose totemic connection to the gods was the once-ubiquitous bison, the destruction of this sacred linkage caused the almost immediate dissolution of tribal identity.* The lesson is clear: When a group or an individual experiences the overwhelmment of its mythic map, the center cannot hold; and the more complex destroys the simpler almost immediately.**

While I was growing up I often heard the phrase "nervous breakdown," as if the nerves had literally broken down. Like the word *neurosis*, coined by the Scottish physician William Cullen in the late eighteenth century, a "nervous breakdown" is a metaphor based on a mechanical, biological model. Nerves do not break down, but our "maps" do. Anyone who has suffered a profound rebuff to his or her values, presumptions, expectations, is susceptible, as much as aboriginal peoples, to the collapse of an idea to which, consciously or unconsciously, they were in service, and in return for which their anxiety was managed and their needs putatively met. On both the personal and the cultural level,

---

* See, for example, N. Scott Momaday's *The Way to Rainy Mountain*, which tracks this cascading tribal dissolution by way of both scholarly detail and his grandmother's oral account.

** A literary example will be found in Goethe's *Faust*, where the complex Faust invades the world of a simple peasant girl, Margaret, and destroys her life map, leading to her suicide. A rare counterexample is found in the film *Witness*, where a jaded Philly detective is redeemed by a simpler Amish culture whose values his soul has missed, though he had not consciously known what he was lacking.

when the ego-center cannot hold, when the historic link-ages to transcendent ground are severed, ego consciousness often implodes upon itself.*

A so-called nervous breakdown is the flooding of the psyche by an overwhelming onslaught of experience, especially experience discordant with ego expectations. Post-traumatic stress disorder, of which we hear much today, is a flooding of psychic resources by a traumatically overwhelming level of energy, as if a nine-volt battery is jammed with a hundred volts of experience. The flashbacks, somatic symptoms, or panic attacks of PTSD are a periodic breakdown of psyche's resources by reactivation of that overwhelming affect. All of us have our limitations, and life can and will overwhelm them from time to time. When one has a supportive circle, the compassion rather than the derision of others, or a linkage to transcendent experience, one recovers a map of the world and reorients one's journey sooner. Many find that the map by which they orient their lives now has to be larger and include more than seemed necessary theretofore. Most of us knit and heal, and sometimes are even stronger for the breaking, and some of us cannot.

REGRESSION

In moments of spiritual crisis we naturally fall back upon what worked for us, or seemed to work, heretofore. Sometimes this shows up through the reassertion of our old values in belligerent, testy ways. Regression of any kind is just such

---

* As the old advice has it, "When in trouble and in doubt, run in circles, scream, and shout."

a return to old presumptions, often after they have been shown to be insufficient for the complexity of larger questions. The virtue of the old presumptions is that they once worked, or seemed to work, and therein lies if not certainty, then nostalgia for a previous, presumptive security. In our private lives, we frequently fall back upon our old roles. I recall a woman who experienced a loss of identity when her children grew up and left home. When her daughter had an early, unexpected baby, she was inordinately thrilled to return to the role of "mother," which had satisfied her twenties but now conveniently allowed her to avoid the developmental tasks of her fifties. This is an example of what Jung called "the regressive restoration of the persona," namely, the re-identification with a former position, role, ideology because it offers a predictable content, security, and script. In the face of the new and uncertain, we often return to the old place, which is why we so often stop growing. (It has become clear to me, for example, that aging itself does not bring wisdom. It often brings regression to childishness, dependency, and bitterness over lost opportunities. Only those who are still intellectually, emotionally, spiritually growing inherit the richness of aging.)

Others gravitate toward groups and fold their hesitant personal authority into the collective ideology. Finding what is true for oneself, and living it in the world, is surely the largest challenge of the second half of life; yet everywhere I look, in large congregations, in small groups, in private therapy, I see people shunning their greatest opportunity, to find and live their own truth. Such persons are denied the rich discovery that our separate, personal, unique journeys, our individuation projects, provide.

Similarly, fundamentalisms of all kinds—political, psychological, theological—offer the sweet promise of certainty, of resolution of ambiguity, and of strict instructions on how to live one's life. It is not a question of anyone's right to believe whatever he or she wishes—that is a given—it is rather that the secret fuel of fundamentalisms of any kind is *fear*—fear of others, fear of challenging, dialectical values, fear of change. While these fears are natural enough, and common to us all, when they prevail they lead to intolerance and even violence, as a casual look at the front page of the newspaper will reveal every day. What I cannot accept in myself, what I cannot handle in the complexity of the world, what I fear in you, often leads me to repress you if I can. Regression, which we all suffer from time to time, is an abrogation of our summons to bring life more fully into the world, to risk being who we are, and to accept the gift that our differences add to the collective.

DISTRACTIONS

We live in a culture replete with distractions. In the seventeenth century mathematician/theologian Blaise Pascal noted in his *Penseés* that contemporary culture invented the jester to distract the king from his sufferings. King though he be, Pascal observed, he grows miserable quickly when left alone in the presence of his own soul. Thus, the jester contrives to amuse the king, divert the court, provide distractions from the awesome magnitude of this journey. What would Pascal think today of our popular media, our video games, our sordid soap operas, tawdry sitcoms, or the Internet with its virtual realities, which similarly serve to fill the awful burden of our days and seduce our terrible freedom? What does it say that a culture invents "reality shows," provides home-shopping networks and dating extravaganzas? Has it become so terrible, as Jean-Paul Sartre predicted, to be free? Are we so spiritually diminished, so enervated, to suffer our crises of the soul in such trivializing fashion?

NARCOTICS

In addition to the sundry distractions of popular culture, which have a narcotizing effect, we have ample availability of substances through which humankind has always sought relief. Our crisis of obesity is ample evidence that the most materially abundant society in history feeds neither the soul nor enlists the spirit. Whatever the soul is looking for will not be found in our pantries and refrigerators. (I do, however, have a few respected comrades who will swear that chocolate provides a path to the sacred.)

Far more subtle than substances is the use of ideologies as anodynes. In 1939 Jung gave a speech to the Guild for Pastoral Psychology in London, just before the outbreak of the war. He noted that, in the words of T. S. Eliot, "humankind cannot bear very much reality." So huge masses drifted to the left to embrace communism, and others to the right to embrace fascism. These herding instincts have always been and will remain with us, for the gift of the group is that one is allowed to relinquish the terrible burden of individual conscience and the struggle of discernment to which every thoughtful person is obliged. Far better to lift one's arm in salute to the leader than to live vexatious questions that oblige one to step away from the mass into the intimidating freedom of our own possibility.

The hope of the future, Jung concluded, will be found in the merely "neurotic," namely, in those souls who have internalized, and are suffering, those questions of meaning of their time and of their personal lives. From these souls, pathways through the forest of ideologies may be found. Let us admit that these same summonses to group identification are still with us. The fascist mind is omnipresent in our country and in our world. But the far more compelling ideologies of our age are materialism, hedonism, and narcissism. (What the Islamic world and the Eastern cultures have most feared is now upon them—the seductive power of distractive materialism. How much easier it is to be distracted by a shiny new object, an easeful comfort, than to search for or serve the gods. No wonder their fundamentalist reactions have been so violent. One is only militant against that which already has a secret foothold in one's psyche.) Yet how little these material fantasies engage the soul, and what diminished gifts they bring to our journeys, is already clear enough, which is why we cling to them so fervently. If materialism, hedonism, narcissism worked for us, really worked, we would know it by now.

TRANSFORMATION

The unbidden gift our spiritual crises can bring to us is the possibility of transformation. In the face of the exhaustion of the old we may 1) find a higher, more evolved form of the old myth; 2) move to a more compelling myth; 3) live without myth, as one's myth; or 4) begin one's journey to a new place.

I am, of course, using the word *myth* here in an honorific sense, namely, as *an energy-charged image, or idea, that has the power to move and direct the soul,* hopefully in ways that link us more deeply to the mysteries of the cosmos, of nature, of relationship, and of self. Mythic systems, whether tribal, collective, or personal, convey images that arise from transcendent encounters—whether with the gods, natural events, the mystery we bring to each other in relationship, or the depths we find within ourselves. As we have seen earlier, to continue to focus on that image, rather than the mystery that gave it life, will in time lead to idolatry. It is the nature of nature to transform itself; energy inevitably leaves that image and elides into newer venues. Whether on the personal or the collective level, we seldom rejoice in this change. Cultures are stultified as they cling to earlier religious images, scientific pictures, cultic customs. On the personal level, we outgrow the previous stages of our development all the time, but how many of us have had to be pulled kicking and screaming into the next stage of life? How many of us have been knocked to our knees before we paid attention? Who, after all, wants to grow up?

As with all other forms of nature, psyche is forever growing, ever evolving. As we have seen, the ego is stuck in gear, resists change, and thus we are often dismayed to find that "the good" now proves the enemy of "the better." Sometimes we are able to move willingly to a more complex, more sophisticated version of the old images. Sometimes we have to leave the old values because our soul has outgrown them. (A friend once said that this is like rowing one's boat to the center of the lake and then stepping out of it. Who would *willingly* do that?) And sometimes we have to live with uncertainty for a very long time until we find a higher purchase on mystery's mountain.

Most often I find people come into therapy because their old map, their former myth, has been exhausted. Recall the solemn utterance of one of my examiners in Zürich who, in the middle of an oral final, said, "My individuation began the day my god died." Each of us respected the gravity of her expression, and of course, knew well what she meant, for all of us had been driven toward a new relationship to the mysteries, to the transforming gods, out of the exhaustion of the old. When Nietzsche professed the death of God in the nineteenth century, he saw persons serving institutional forms, rote expressions, received confessions, ritualized behavior, but no joy, no transformation, no mystery. He understood that when something is psychologically dead, it is also spiritually dead, though the dead may continue walking in their sleep for decades, and even pass on this spiritual somnambulism to their descendants. Nietzsche tried to create a more compelling myth, the myth of Zarathustra, the *Übermensch*,* but one cannot spin myth out of one's consciousness any more than from a committee. Myth comes from below, from the unconscious, from the telluric gods, from the earth. When he went mad in his last years, his enemies cheaply critiqued his heroic efforts to take the life of the spirit seriously and slurred his apparent atheism. In fact, he was suffering the terminal phase of general paresis, but in my view Nietzsche lived his life with more passion, emotional honesty, and

---

* Literally, the *Overman*, the Superior Man, by which he meant the evolved, conscious human. The later perverse misappropriation of this term by Nazi ideologues ignored the fact that Nietzsche demanded that individual consciousness spurn the herd, as well as the many occasions where he denounced anti-Semitism as the lowest form of ignorance.

spiritual vitality than all of his conservative critics combined.

Others seek to live without myth, as if one could. Though we may disdain someone else's myth, we are never myth-free, for we all swim in "myth-streams." We are assaulted daily by seductive energies from popular culture, and succumb or resist or transcend them according to the level of our consciousness. When people say to me that they live without myth, then I know that they are unaware that most of our lives are in service to those splinter myths we call *complexes*. Complexes are fractal forms, charged with energies, compelling scripts, admonitions, and outcomes, which is why so much of our histories reveal patterns even though we righteously presume and proclaim our freedoms. No one lives without myth. Anyone who thinks so is very unconscious. The only question is what mythologems, what fragments, what admonitions, what retreats or flights, what tropic desires have sovereignty in our lives and make our choices for us.

Sooner or later, we all outgrow the previous map, the myth to which we were in service, whether knowingly or not. These moments, these internodal moments, can be extremely painful, but they point either to the inadequacy of our map to effectively describe the terrain we traverse, or represent an inner, compelling summons of the soul to grow and develop a better one. This very day I spoke with a woman who had lost a thirty-year-plus marriage and also heard of a couple lose a newborn. Each was suffering the loss of hope, expectation, investment, and sincere desire. No one who goes through such suffering can know what lies beyond this valley of the shadow of death. But we all, unless we are suddenly erased from the ranks of the living, are thrust into newer worlds whether we wish to be or not. As the medieval proverb had it, "Suffering is the fastest horse to completion." No one wants to go there, but as one John Lennon observed, life is what happens when we had other plans.

Transformation often comes to us in symbolic form. We have a dream image that perplexes, a symptom that will not go away, a relational pattern that continues to fester—each of these is a summons to ask: *What does the soul want of me?* Notice that this transformation has little if anything to do with the ego's comfort or control, or the approval of others. To ask what the soul wants of me is to submit to what "the gods"* wish, investing themselves through the energies of the individual psyche, energies that are transcendent to ordinary ego consciousness. To serve the gods, not the ego, not the tribe, not one's parents, not one's prior picture, is to *transform*.

People have misunderstood Jung's "myth for our time," *individuation*, as narcissism or self-preoccupation. In fact it is a summons to service, of ego submission to values larger than those previously embraced. In his book *Fear and Trembling*, Danish theologian Søren Kierkegaard wrestles with what he calls "the scandal of Abraham and Isaac." How could one in conscience sacrifice his child, even to the summons of a god? What we find in this puzzling parable is rather the paradox that to serve the transcendent we are sometimes obliged to sacrifice whatever we theretofore most valued. There is little comfort to the ego on such occasions, but one is brought to spiritual enlargement.

---

* Remember that the metaphor *the gods* refers not to supernatural beings, as such, but to our respect for those purposive energies that course through the cosmos, and through each of us.

Many times, against our will, we find that in our crises and other bad days at the office there is an enlargement of the spirit purchased by suffering and humility, but enlargement nonetheless. The death of our myth, the experience of meaninglessness, is the beginning of a new stage, the next stage, of our journey. Not what we had in mind, perhaps, but fate or the soul—perhaps they are often the same—has another intent: that we begin the move to another phase of our journey and a revisioning of our values. We may like it less at first, but we will be larger for going there.

Chapter Ten

THAT WE WRITE OUR STORY, LEST SOMEONE ELSE WRITE IT FOR US

"One is oneself the biggest of all one's assumptions, and the one with the gravest consequences."

"The Practice of Psychotherapy," C. G. Jung

"Each mortal thing does one thing and the same:
Deals out that being indoors each one dwells:
Selves—goes itself; myself it speaks and spells,
Crying What I do is me: for that I came.

"As Kingfishers Catch Fire," G. M. Hopkins

*W*e spend our lives amid furious collisions of outer and inner imperatives, energies, agendas. Finding our personal thread amid this plethora of cables, knots, and networks is our task, and is especially the mission that psychoanalysis undertakes. While the corporeal eye is seduced by the world of appearances, mere facticities, invisible energies govern that visible world, which is why it is so difficult for any of us to become wholly, or even partly, conscious on a sustained basis.

Every life is an enactment of stories, the sum of which is our biography, our résumé, our epitaph. But the story we tell ourselves, or others, is only the story of which we are conscious. Our more enduring, more pervasive stories rise from deep, very deep archetypal matrices, genetic predispositions, cultural forms, intergenerational messages, sundry reflexive, reactive readings, and acquired defenses amid a world essentially unknowable, sometimes hostile, from which we do not escape alive. Nonetheless, we are called to achieve personhood—to contribute most to others by becoming who we are, and standing for values that matter in this world, whatever the obstacles history provides us.

As a psychoanalyst, my daily work is to "read" surfaces— what we say, what we do not say, what the body proclaims, what the behaviors serve, what the dream images intimate, and so on. But, even more, it is to "read" what these outer forms intimate of a simultaneous inner drama. Daily, we embody complex, competitive, and compelling narratives that are mysterious, elusive, and by and large autonomous. It is disturbing to think that rather than we living our stories, *our stories might be living us.* Our precious, self-deluding ego, necessary for choice and responsible for consequences, is so often a vassal of compelling narratives that swirl upward from the unconscious, yet is obliged to respond as effectively as it can to the reality demands of its environment. To acknowledge that there are genetic codes, archetypally formative patterns, and fractal psychic scripts to which we are in service, is humbling at best and frequently intimidating, especially when life asks more of us than we feel capable of providing. While there are conscious stories we claim as ours, unconscious stories we enact every day prove over time even more intimately ours. Additionally, there is a larger story of humanity to which we contribute our small chapters in unique but patterned ways.

If I were to ask you, "What is your story?" I would more properly need to ask you, "What are your stories?" for you are no single narrative, plot line, denouement, cast of characters, or simple meaning. If Hamlet proved complex, and he is still riddling the critics after four centuries, let them consider the copious conundrums that any one of our lives embody. Hamlet is only a literary character, limited always to the text he was given by some guy presumably named Shakespeare. But what of you? You contain a Hamlet "story" or "complex"; namely, there are times when you know what you should do, but for reasons you do not know, you do not or cannot do what you know you should do. Yet, unlike Hamlet, you are not limited to a script. Unlike Hamlet, you can choose new lines, new directions for your life. You can rewrite the whole script, change the plotline, rewrite the denouement. Or can you?

Recently a journalist interviewed me for an article. Why would a person come into analytic therapy if not to "solve a problem"? she reasonably asked. Well, often people do come to analysis because they have a problem—a troubling marriage, a resistant depression, an addictive pattern, a loss of direction. While not ignoring a presenting "problem," a psychodynamic approach rather seeks to discern what role such problems play in the larger story of our lives. Thus the goal of an analytic therapy is not a "solution" to life's problems—were even a solution to exist—but to find one's story more interesting, to find that each of us is, after all, a character of great depth amid a deeply coursing drama, filled with life-defining choices presented on a daily basis. At first glance, to make one's story more "interesting" does not appear to help a person in great pain at the moment, but all of our lives are an unfolding mystery in which we are both intimately involved and amazed witnesses. Achieving a more conscious participation in a richer story proves a great gift after all. (Synchronistically, a friend e-mailed me a cartoon showing a therapist saying to a client, "Look, making you happy is out of the question, but I can give you a compelling narrative for your misery.")

We are all, to ourselves and others, a deep autonomous mystery, the progressive incarnation of which occurs in the most modest, the most horrifying, the most humbling of moments. Our sojourn on this planet is brief, indeed, and yet we are unique carriers of the energies of the cosmos. Whatever our small role, it is vital, integral to the whole, for no mosaic exists apart from its brilliant, separate parts. So our aggregate stories are our lives, living us as much as we live them, and always part of a larger, much larger story.

IT BEGINS IN WONDER

Your story is wrapped around and within the world story, and the world story is enfolded within your private story. Do you not recall in childhood the primal sense of wonder about who you were, who made the world, what it was all about? We were never more fully human than in those moments of great, gracious, and enlarging questions.

But consider what your operative "questions" may be today: "How can I be financially secure?" "How can I convince my children to endorse my values?" "How can I find a partner to meet my needs?" or "How can I get someone to take care of me?" Do these questions enlarge us, or do they diminish us? Do their answers provide sustained satisfaction?

Do our questions infantilize us, or do they ask that we *grow up* by, paradoxically, returning to the questions that primal wonder first occasioned for us as children?

The questions we ask, implicitly or explicitly, define our story for us. If they are, as they were so often for the world of our parents, "How do I get people to like me, accept me?" chances are we have learned to be a *bricoleur*, a juggler of sorts who twists, turns, deflects, and manages to divert entertainingly in service to the plaudits of the other. If our question is, "How do I find security?" chances are our story is fear-based, and thus abiding security is always farther and farther away.* If our question is, "How do I avoid offending God?" or "How do I get God on my side?" the more we may offend divinity by not being who we were meant to be, or the more manipulative we become in contriving a delusive "deal" with the universe.

The implicit, and sometimes explicit, questions our family of origin asked, or our tribe or culture asks, become our questions by default, and we either serve their provisional answers, rebel against them, or try unconsciously to resolve them. Either way we are still in service to someone else's questions, someone else's answers, someone else's unresolved relationship to the universe.

Without speaking of it till now, I recall as a child of five to seven reflecting on the source of all this stuff, this wondrous

---

* I am reminded of this paradox during this troubled time of America when the more we invest in a fortress psychology—safe, secure, and highly bordered from all others—the less and less secure we feel. The higher the walls I build, the more imprisoned by fear I am. Whether fences are physical or psychological, they fence me in. The more we invest in transportation security or homeland defense, the more constrained we are by our fears, and the more costly to both purse and psychology.

world so construed, so imagined. I fantasized that the cloud-capped vault of the skies I saw above me formed a cell, perhaps a globe, and that that cell was a part of the brain of a giant person, a thinker, a dreamer, and that I and the world I perceived about me was a thought of that thinker, or its dream. It subsequently occurred to me that that thinker might have another thought, or wake from the dream, and that I and my world might disappear. Strangely I did not tell anyone of this parabolic image for I feared condemnation or ridicule, both of which I had already encountered in sufficient measure for such thoughts. Strangely, I was not frightened by this cosmic fantasy, despite the insubstantial purchase on longevity it offered me. Rather I was fascinated by it. This image helped me relate through wonder to an amazing universe, and abides with me still, for I am still aware that that thinker might have another thought, that dreamer might awaken to another dream.* That childhood fantasy lingers because it deepens. In its infinite regressions of wonder it brings mystery and a richer story.

All children ask these questions, even as it is clear that by the time we are adults, most of us have lost contact with primal wonder, been shamed or intimidated into silence, and are fractionated into roles with all their attendant scenarios. How resonant it was to later encounter James Agee's roman à clef, or autobiographical novel, *A Death in the Family*, which recounts the pain and wonder of a child when his father is killed in an auto accident. The opening sentence of this novel alerts us to the fact that the quotidian debris of

---

* In a parallel fantasy, Jung recounts sitting on a stone as a child, wondering whether he was "thinking" the stone, or the stone was "thinking" him.

our daily lives always takes place in the larger context of wonder. "We are talking now of summer evenings in Knoxville, Tennessee, in the time that I lived there so successfully disguised to myself as a child."*

That sentence has always grabbed me. Clearly the child is present to the largeness of his journey, as I believe we all once were, and his sensibility is attuned to the great mystery of the evening skies and his enigmatic place in it. His body is small, but his imagination large. He wonders what has brought him and his family members together to this place, this moment. "By some chance here they all are, all on this earth; and who shall ever tell the sorrow of being on this earth, lying, on quilts, on the grass, in a summer evening, among the sounds of the night. . . . After a little while I am taken in and put to bed . . . and those receive me, who quietly treat me, as one familiar and well beloved in that home: but will not, oh, will not, not now, not ever; but will not ever tell me who I am."** For Agee, wonder presents itself through the question "Who am I?" He is his mother's son, his father's orphan, but the question abides, for we all know we are more than our relationships, our roles, our functions—but what are we, then?

For the person with a high sensate function—the engineer, systems analyst, troubleshooter, accountant—the question is "How do the pieces best fit together?" For the pragmatist, for whom ideas are merely instruments, the question is "How well does it work, and what are the payoffs?" For the aesthetic sensibility the question presents as "What is

* James Agee, *A Death in the Family*, p. 11.

** *Ibid.*, p. 15.

its texture?" "What color or form appeals to me?" "What would it look like if I moved something over here instead?" All of these questions are expressions of primal wonder and represent a desire to connect with the invisible world that informs and drives the visible world.

If, however, our prevailing questions are "How can I be secure?" or "Where can I find protective love?" or "How can I be liked by everyone?" then one is enslaved to the responses of others. In granting authority and empowerment to the external world we remain all the more at the mercy of its vagaries. (As a colleague said to a client once, "In your relationships you sacrificed your autonomy to gain security and wound up with neither.") Each of these questions, understandable as they are, are in service to security rather than wonder, and therefore diminish our stories.

James Agee, for example, returned to the pivotal event of his father's death and sought to find its meaning for him. He wrote and rewrote his manuscript at least seven times and was still not finished with it when death took him in 1955. While he delineates the response of each family member to the death of Jay, the father, the axis around which everything turns is always: "And who am I?"

The Prague-born poet Rainer Maria Rilke similarly dredged his childhood memories for the vital threads of psychological continuity that hold us together in so many disparate settings. What was real, what persists, what still nurtures in the congeries of events we summon from the vaults of memory? In his mind's eye he recalls the lost playgrounds of childhood, and the little friends with whom he cavorted. Their spontaneous joys, their innocence, their sudden frights and flights, their exuberance, are all effaced by time, by narrowing corridors of memory, until, fretted by adult gravities, the linkage to their secret self is lost. What was real, then, in the flood of sensations, the concatenations of events, the flush and flurry of flung bodies?

> *What was real in all that?*
> *Nothing. Only the balls, with their wonderful curves.*
> *Not even the children . . . for sometimes one of them,*
> *Oh fleeting child, stepped under a falling ball.**

With marvelous economy of language, Rilke summons forth the huge affect still tied to these images from childhood. The ball at the heart of so many childhood games serves not only as a literal memory, but as a metonymy for the curve of time and space back upon us. The ball, thrown ever so high, ever so far, will, must, always, return to earth—as do we. So these mortal children—aspirant to Heaven but gravity bound—forever arc back to earth. And, as this ball spins forth from the hall of memory, its shadow covers our whole planet, another falling ball, upon which we spend our fugitive, fleeting days.

In his selection of the image of the ball, both childhood game and metonymy for the curve of our common condition, Rilke succeeds not only in his recollection of childhood, but remembers the mortal purchase with which we cling to another, larger spinning ball we call our planet. Each of us, though at play for the moment, steps finally into the curving career of things human. That is our common story, our common destiny, our common gravitas.

* Rainer Maria Rilke, *The Sonnets to Orpheus*, II, 8. Author's translation.

So think on those moments in your recollected back-
yard, in the south field, in the street, the park. What did
you think when alone with your thoughts, then? What did you
imagine? What spectral fears harried you? When you lay in
bed at night, what strange animals growled beneath you,
what groaning critters paced in your closet? By day my
brother Alan and I pulled on the mattress springs under our
twin beds and raced on our backs amid the dust balls, back
and forth, in never-ending heats of childhood Olympics. By
night alligators lurked beneath those same beds. Never mind
that no alligators had ever been seen in Illinois; they were
there, as we knew from Tarzan movies, waiting to munch
on the limbs of careless children. In those days, a passing
plane was enough of an event to bring us out of the house to
watch in wonder as it flew over. I deeply longed to fly someday and to go where those silvery silhouettes took one. I try
to remember that wonder these days with TSA delays and
endless airport lines. But flying is still a wonder, and it is still
a compelling part of my story.

In our childhoods, events of the future hurtled toward us
as surely as December, but we could not see them. We wondered if we would be worthy of what loomed before us. We
wondered if "they," the Big Folks, would take us aside, finally,
and tell us what it was all about. While Fate, goddess of limits,
hedged us from every side, Choice, real or imagined, con-
tended with her for sovereignty, and we enacted our stories
unconsciously. We earnestly, sometimes desperately "read"
events, other people's models, whatever we could learn of
what our story was about, how it was to be played, and how it
was to end. When we reached high school, something called
puberty descended upon us, or better, rose from our loins,

and the body grew, archaic, anarchic and insistent, even as we knew we were still children thrust now into an adult arena.

So, still today, we look back down the highway, seeing the wreckage, the carnage of hope, the bent dreams, the many casualties taken, the heart's collateral damage. We wish to blame someone for all this, although we grudgingly admit that the only person present in all those passing scenes has been ourselves, and so somehow we must be accountable before our history. By now most of us have figured out that the Big Folks did not know, though some of them certainly acted as if they did. Our story, with its many sub-stories, still courses through us, and we are still trying to figure out what it is, what it means, and what we are to do about it.

In speaking of these matters in a public setting recently, someone said, "Why should I bother to think about these things?" "Well, because perhaps you are living someone else's story if you do not," I replied. "What does that matter if I'm happy?" she retorted. "Though I am not against happiness," I returned, "I do consider it to be a poor measure of the worth and depth of one's life. Throughout history, the people who brought us the most often suffered greatly, and were scarcely happy carrots."* Thus endeth our conversation. I did have the lingering impression that she did not want to work very hard at this identity stuff. I also know that our psyches will not be mocked and that somewhere deep within something profound gets wounded and ultimately reaches the surface as symptom, projection, obsession, or some form of pathology.**

---

* I owe the phrase "happy carrots" to Joan Siracusa of Ventnor, NJ.

** The word *pathology* literally means "the expression of suffering."

Avoiding researching our story, claiming its paradoxes and contradictions as ours, is the chief preoccupation of modern life—a culture of addiction, distraction, and numbing. This flight from engaging our stories constitutes *mauvais foi*, or bad faith, to Jean-Paul Sartre, inauthentic being as "sin" to Paul Tillich, and as neurosis to depth psychology. Another way of expressing this estrangement from ourselves is that we have forgotten our stories, or perhaps accepted someone else's version, or have consigned authorship to those energy-laden complexes that run their splinter narratives ceaselessly.

THE PROVISIONAL STORY

As we saw in the first chapter, we all, because of our dependency and lack of consciousness, resign our deepest stories, that is, the stories intended by the gods, and trade them in for the provisional stories that our reading of the world around us provides. We pick up the stories of others; we internalize the messages of family of origin and popular culture, and progressively lose the narrative thread of our story. Wordsworth recognized this phenomenon more than two centuries ago when he wrote his famous poem "Ode on Intimations of Immortality." The infant enters this plane, he describes, "trailing clouds of glory," but the iterations, demands, contingencies of daily life cause the connection to the transcendent to "fade into the light of common day" by adolescence. Someone else's story supplants ours and our individuation summons is replaced by another narrative.

Recovering our story, risking it, is what Jung meant by the *individuation* project. Because we get wrapped within our provisional stories, the received scripts, we necessarily serve the compelling imagoes they embody. Archaic intra-psychic imagoes of self and other predispose us to repetitions in relationship. Or we bump up against the glass ceiling of familial limitations, the constricted imagination of complexes, or the constraints of tribal claim upon us. How much of our daily life, our unfolding story, is driven by such ghostly search engines whose origins are found, in Shakespeare's phrase, in "the dark backward and abysm of time"?

In the womb, the lungs did not breathe, the eyes did not see, and we floated timelessly through inner space. Time, consciousness, identity are the epiphenomena of a splitting into opposites occasioned by our birth. The prerequisite for consciousness and identity is suffering, the suffering of radical separation, the splitting of subject and object, the loss of connection. No wonder all peoples have their founding myths expressing loss, separation from a "paradisal state," and no wonder we resist consciousness so much. When we further find our dependency absolute, vulnerability total, we learn to adapt our narrative to whatever imperative presents itself as most insistent. So we grow separated from our story. Later, perhaps reading the story of others, we learn that there are alternatives.*

Just this day I was discussing with a woman how she learned patterns of avoidance in dealing with conflictual circumstances. Child of a rageaholic mother and a compliant father, she had no other model, no other strategy apparent. Her

---

* As a child, I devoured biographies. I hungered to learn how their subjects saw the world differently, how they broadened our range of choices by their actions, and how they opened my tiny world to at least include their story along with mine.

reflexive application of an avoidant pattern over the course of her adult life, however, led to quite troubling circumstances: a domineering husband and a self-sabotaging passivity with her children and coworkers. Fortunately, alternative choices modeled by others whom she admires, the compensatory messages of her dreams, and her progressive accumulation of ego strength have brought this fiftysomething woman to a place where she is choosing more grounded positions of personal integrity, despite the opposition of others.

Recall that mere recognition of these primal, acquired, provisional stories does not mean that they go away, or are even depotentiated, however. The earlier the story, the more powerfully reinforced and the greater its staying power; the narrative wiring goes directly to our dank basement where catastrophic consequences retain their veto power. The unconscious, archaic but "catastrophic thought" says, for example, "If you resist the other, they will destroy you—either you will be harmed; or you will be abandoned." Such prospects would obviously prove devastating to the child, and even now, they remain troubling to the adult. The guardians at the gates of our freedom are still large and intimidating.

How difficult is it for us to change our stories by taking "counter-phobic steps" as correctives? How often do we see someone's life devoted to compliance, hoping to curry favor and avoid retribution? How often do we see someone repeatedly miring themselves in bad relationships, hoping to wrest love, security, affirmation at last? How often do we see people transferring their infantile needs to substances, to power, to sex, or seeking to redo their lives, and avoid responsibility for addressing the next stage of their own development, by attaching to their children or grandchildren?

How difficult is it for us to reclaim our journeys by moving toward, rather than away from, our fearful places? As philosopher Martin Heidegger said once, "the *Terrible* has already happened." But in the timeless realm of the core complexes, catastrophic messages retain their sovereign and timeless power. How courageous one must be, thereby, to stand up against these disempowering messages and reclaim one's story. Surely the supreme task of the second half of life requires taking on accountability for writing one's personal story and the acquisition of courage to live it in the world. As the old Zen koan has it, "What was the face you had before the world was made?" Those venerable sages knew that the story the ego was living, the fiction it embraced, was not the true story, hence the deep sorrow, the nostalgia we all carry for a lost home. *That lost home is ourselves.* How do we ever make it back there? Paradoxically, we can only make it back home to ourselves by going forward into the unknown, scary possibilities of a risky, more fully lived journey. Each of us is aware of many places where our story beckons, and we have been so for a very long time, but we have mostly managed to avoid stepping into it.

GOING HOME: A STORY

How does one go home, without going back to an earlier place, a place that cannot be recovered, and whose delusory seduction leads to regression? In using the word *nostalgia* (which from the Greek means "pain for home") above, one risks the seduction of sentimentality, of returning to a safe, familiar psychology, and of staying stuck in someone else's story. Perhaps the most seductive of all "going home" fantasies is to find the "magical Other," through whom we are nurtured, protected, kept from the journey.* Whatever our story may be, and that is for us to discover, it will require suffering, risk, anxiety, and often great loneliness. No wonder we prefer the simpler past.

So, how do we go forward to recover home, the one the gods intended? Recently, a man had the following dream.

> As a student in a college course, I went to see the male instructor . . . but he was in a meeting, so I left.
>
> I walked about the campus on my own. On the gravel walk I noticed what looked like an old beat-up teakettle without handle or lid. I examined it. Inside there was a glint of silver in the hay. I found a few coins covered with rusty water. At the bottom of the pot were three sets of keys on chains—seven keys on each chain. Underneath these sets were many unattached keys of all kinds. I took the three chains and two large handfuls of separate keys and put them in my pockets.

That is where the dream ends. Who would make up this stuff, and from where?** What I find remarkable about this dream is how it reflects from within upon the continuing departure of this man from received authorities of others toward the discovery of his personal authority.

---

* Let us be clear that while "romance," along with materialism, parades as the chief elixir for alienated modernism, it is not the only venue in which this fantasy may abide. Ideologies, theologies, institutions—all seemingly offer the fantasy of connection, surcease, and satiety. Thereby our vessel never leaves home port, never sails turbulent seas, never discovers what waits for us to discover.

** Jungian analyst Robert Johnson told the story of a man who "made up" his dreams in order to sabotage the therapeutic process. When Johnson pointed out that all the contrived motifs were in fact part of this man's story, he burst into tears, and the therapy became real at last.

(There may be others from whom we can learn alternative stories—that is the most useful service that parents, teachers, mentors, and therapists can offer, but we cannot find our authority to live our journey, and encounter the mystery of this journey, through them. We have to find that from within some more authentic narrative that is already written deeply within our psyches. Remember Hölderlin's observation, that what we seek is near, and already coming to meet us.)

The dreamer was not especially conscious of the archetypal import of the numbers three and seven,* whose histories track through millennia of religious, mythological, and cultural patterns, but he certainly understands the encounter with the mystery that beckons him from within that kettle. Whether the kettle is the witches' pot, or the alchemist's alembic, it is the container for brewing the materials of his larger spiritual life, where the whole equals more, much more, than the sum of its parts. But he, and we, surely understand the metaphor of *keys*. What is to be unlocked for us in the outer world; what is to be unlocked for us in our inner world? There are keys, keys aplenty—our bodies; our intuitions; our conscious, patient, sorting reflections; and our compensatory dreams, symptoms, visions.

The keys are always there; they always have been, but we learned to distrust them while adapting to and obeying the clamorous claims of the world. But seen or not seen, they are always there, announcing a summons to open our journeys to a larger world. When such keys are neglected, something in the soul dies, goes underground and grieves, or enters the

---

* The number *three* historically suggests change, transformation, spilling over into the balanced opposites that the four embodies. *Seven* then is the three and the four, the older integration moving through a developmental dynamic toward a still higher resolution. This archetypal arcana need not be known to consciousness to be working still in our unconscious dynamics.

outer world as a projection that tricks the eye, diverts us into empty amusements or distractions, or sends us chasing spiritual will-o'-the-wisps. In fact, we can say that a central principle of psychic life is: *Whatever is excluded from our psychic reality will go underground as pathological grieving, namely, depression, or will enter the world via projection, and seduce and enslave us with futile efforts to capture and hold finally what forever eludes our grasp.*

"Going home" means paying attention to, respecting, the witness of these clues. It asks that we risk taking them seriously. It means tracking the clues to see where they wish to take us, which will not necessarily be where we wish to go. Going home means coming back to ourselves after so much estrangement. So long have we been strangers in this world, and so long strangers to ourselves. How scary, how inviting, how necessary it is to come home at last.

Let me conclude this chapter on the writing of our stories by quoting, with permission, the story of one person whom I know who has always marched to the beat of another drummer, paid his dues, and lived with an integrity of ethical, relational values and commitments seldom seen in this compromised, fallen world. He asks that we look at our lives, consider what chip we are supposed to bring to the mosaic of the universe, and then step forth on our own journey, writing our own story.

> *Ethic*
> *I have always believed in a strong work ethic*
> *but the definition of which is widely different:*
> *I didn't do well in school;*
> *I have gone job to job,*
> *but what I worked on most,*

*the only thing I care about,
is being the best human being I can be.*

*This is in conflict with number crunchers,
those who still believe in a ladder to success.
I failed miserably in all those respects
and have a genuine friend from each of those experiences.*

*The definitions put forth in this culture, and many others,
work well for those like minded:
for those of us who are centered elsewhere
it often ends poorly.*

*I know the routines very well and have performed,
but when I see an antlered buck on the side of the road
or a rock that sparks fascination,
or a grocer who is especially kind,
I feel alive.*

*Of course we need bridge builders and planners
and those with heart-mind of creating community,
and I think I am not an aberration
but a necessary part.*

*I do not advocate anyone follow my path:
there is a place, though,
for the mystical, the artists, poets and the like
        to stop, for a second, the serious minded
        and say, "look."*

---

* "Ethic," by Timothy James Hollis, a poem sent to me by e-mail.

Imagine what our story would look like if, rather than succumbing to the insistent voices of family or culture, we determined that our vocation was to be a better human. Many, if not most of us, will have run through our lives and never really been here, never really experienced precious moments of mindfulness, asked *why*, or felt ourselves in the presence of mystery, whether found in the beloved, in nature, in contemplation, in the work of hands, or in whatever venues mystery comes to find us.

The writer above served his journey, lived his story, by bringing ethical values to his congress with others, and even more by asking us to stop and "look" with the eyes of wonder again. Even as a child, he knew in his bones what matters most. Former Illinois governor and UN Ambassador Adlai Stevenson observed that the moral measure of a nation is not found in its GNP, but in how it treats its least-advantaged citizens. This young man knew that what persists after we are gone is seldom what we did, but who one was, the number of people one touched; not what one accumulated, but what is grieved, and by whom, in one's absence.

What matters is that we become who we are, really are. As Jung reminds us:

> Personality is the supreme realization of the innate idiosyncrasy of a living being. It is an act of high courage flung in the face of life. . . . True personality is always a vocation and puts its trust in it as in God, despite its being, as the ordinary man would say, only a personal feeling. But vocation acts like a law of God from which there is no escape. The fact that many a man who goes his own way ends in ruin means nothing to one who has a voca-

tion. He *must* obey his own law. Anyone with a vocation hears the voice of the inner man: he is *called.**

Personhood is not a gift; it is a continuing struggle; the gift is attained later, and only from living a mindful journey where, prompted by an inner summons, we write our story at last.

---

* Jung, *The Development of Personality, CW 17*, pars. 289, 300.

Chapter Eleven

AMOR FATI: THAT WE FIGHT FATE, AND LOVE IT ALSO

". . . the fury and mire of human veins."

W. B. YEATS

*W*e are granted the gift of life, a gift of uncertain duration but of certain travail. However much we lament, protest, negotiate, this short pause is all we get. For many, fate overwhelms, destroys, truncates their journey. Why did one of my best friends, Nelson, die just after college, and why me, the lesser man, live on? Providence? Perhaps, but such a Providence I repudiate and say "no thanks." But can we say "no thanks" to life? Can we ever reconcile how *we* can be here, hovering over the abyss, hanging by the fragile thread of mortality, while others perish? And when is it our turn—we who have been granted the unearned privilege to write (or read) this book?

Those of us who are merely and mostly neurotic are frequently called to recognize that *we* are the primary source of our own suffering. We are divided against ourselves, and frequently stumble over our own estrangements, confusions, and moments of cowardice. As the poet Gerard Manley Hopkins expressed it, we are our own "sweating selves, but worse."

What worse could there be than the knowledge of our collusion with our suffering, and our many dysfunctions? Yes, there are some who are overwhelmed by their fate and categorized by the psychiatric manuals as having "personality disorders." There is a world of difference between *suffering* a wound, and the splits it causes, and *being* wholly governed by that wound. The dilemma of the so-called personality disorders is that the ego, that fragile vessel of consciousness, is owned by the wound and automatically defaults to the historic data of wounding and its message of adaptive survival. Thus the *avoidant personality disorder* survives by separation and repetitive flight. But what costs accrue from a life of flight? The *dependent personality disorder* sacrifices personal authority for security, and never finds either. The *sociopathic personality* survives by brutalizing others, and lives a terrible, perduring, beleaguered isolation as a consequence. The *obsessive-compulsive personality* is terrified by loss of control and thereby enlists urgent management systems, yet can never finally be in charge, for there is always another loose end yet to be covered. The *narcissistic personality disorder* is owned by an anxious desire to find an affirming mirror in the other, for, repeatedly staring into the mirror of self, he or she finds no one smiling back. And so on. These sluggish, recalcitrant, fateful conditions are surely what our ancestors would have called "hell." Such an underworld is peopled by ghost-ridden dreams, constricted imagination, and damnable repetitions.

One crude distinction has been offered: Generally speaking, the *neurotic* is a problem to him/herself, and the *personality disorder* is a problem to others. But as troubling to others as they so often prove to be, these persons suffer such self-estrangement as to be trapped in a world without an aperture into alternative possibility. I recall saying to a woman who finally escaped an abusive relationship with a sociopath: "You are free of him now." "But," she answered, "he never seems to have to deal with the consequences. He always skates off to ruin somebody else's life." "Yes, that seems true, but he always has to live with an emptied soul,* and you don't . . . anymore." I am not at all sure, amid all the carnage, that she appreciated how much better her wounded life was than his. Among her narrow blessings was that she had hope, where he had none; she had choices, where he reflexively defaulted; she had a shred of possibility, where he served enslaving fate. But to what degree do we all serve Fate—share the condition of Sisyphus, condemned to roll the boulder up the hill, only to see it tumble again? Or to what degree do we have some play of freedom, even in the face of fate?

◆ ◆ ◆

Humankind has always lived in an edgy relationship with the gods. The ancient, archetypal imagination intuitively understood energy systems in ways that contemporary physics is only now enabling us to reappropriate. While the nineteenth century utilized the metaphors of *machine* and *matter*, the twentieth privileged metaphors of *information* and *virtual reality*. But the implications of Einstein, Heisenberg, and the developments of quantum physics recovered an energic world of verbs rather than static nouns. Recall also that Heraclitus said it best, and perhaps first: "All is fire." (He understood

---

* I am grateful to Zürich colleague Adolf Güggenbuhl-Craig for this epithet, "the emptied soul," in describing the ravaged inner terrain of the sociopath.

metaphor, for, after all, *metaphor* is a Greek word.) What is "fire" but a metaphor for energy constantly transmogrifying, creating and destroying like Vishnu, and consuming itself as our own bodies do?* So, in dealing with our human condition, we need to observe and respect energy above all, energy that is forever creating, destroying, changing. Knowing that the word *God* summons too many complexes, too many specific associations, or has been entombed as "the stern parent" by fundamentalism, we may be most served by reappropriating the energic metaphor of *the gods* to hold in creative tension a respectful relationship to the transcendent energies that course through all things finite.

Another way of looking at our life is to confess that we swim continuously in force fields of energy. One of those force fields, or energy systems, our Greek ancestors called *Moira*, and the Islamic world *Kismet*, or *Fate*. This is the energy of finite creation, with all its limits, boundaries, confines. You are born a certain person, with a genetic code, a set of parents, a cultural context, a zeitgeist, and in significant proportion are defined and delimited by these realities. At the same time, you swim in a force field they called *proorismos*, or *Destiny*, which is an expanding field of possible outcomes. Destiny encompasses whatever is capable of becoming. And, placed right there at the crossroads of fate and destiny like Oedipus in the wilderness of Cithaeron, is the limited human being with all his or her quite unique dynamics: character, biased vision, and capacity for self-deception.**

---

* Recall also Dylan Thomas's felicitous antinomy, "the force that through the green fuse drives the flower is my destroyer."

** Known to students of the tragic vision as *kharakter*, *hamartia*, and *hubris*.

What has been called "the tragic vision" is not a morbid view of life, but rather a fascinating, intuitive perception made twenty-six centuries before us that the lives we construct are an inextricably woven fabric of influences, possibilities, and accumulated consequences of choices made. Later—much later, if at all—we reluctantly come to recognize that those choices we made were reflective of our character, our limited field of vision, and our presumption that we knew enough to know enough. The "gift" of tragedy is not destruction, but humility after we presumptively assumed informed consciousness and sovereign control of our lives. The end of the tragic vision is to remind us that we never know enough to know enough; yet we are still bound to choose, and always remain responsible for choices made, or choices avoided. What we call "depth psychology" explores the mix of these myriad factors, and is only a later refinement of the primal, intuitive perceptions of our ancestors. Where we have psychology, our predecessors had myths that dramatized both the dynamics and the motifs of the unconscious. Discerning force fields is difficult work, yet they play out daily in our lives, and in our effects upon others. Both the tragic vision and depth therapy provide us lenses through which to see the variegated levels and textures of our history. More important than whether our choices appear "good" or "bad," we are obliged to ask what scripts they are in service to in the energy fields unknown to consciousness.

◆ ◆ ◆

In the last chapter we affirmed the power of stories, our need to make them conscious, and to amend them when we can.

Let us add a layer to this metaphor of "stories." As we saw, each of us has a story; in fact many stories. It is accurate to say that any memory, any reflexive response, any complex activated in us has a story. In one complex, for example, no matter what our age or station in life, the floor on which we confidently stand drops us into our psychic basement, into the presence of a vulnerable child, anxiously soliciting the approval of the other. In another complex, we play the bully who, contrary to our professed values, imposes his will upon the other, replete with ready rationalizations. In still another, no matter how accomplished we may appear to the outer world, we experience ourselves lacking elemental permission to feel what we feel, or desire what we desire. Each of these complexes is a splinter story, a mythological force field, and when we are subsumed by such energized valences, consciously or unconsciously, we make our choices, follow our scripts meticulously. This is the source of those patterns that recur in our lives, despite our notion that we are living freely, consciously, and in accord with our professed values. The fractal energies attached to these stories have the capacity to usurp consciousness, govern the ego for a while, and enlist behaviors in service to history once again. Only the delusion of consciousness, of being wholly in this moment, allows us to deny the many ways we remain in service to the past. As the novelist William Faulkner once observed, the past is not dead; it is not even past.

But beneath all these splinter stories, powerful as they are, other, more comprehensive stories thrum and throb, and surface in so many different venues of our lives. Let me give some examples.

A thirty-eight-year-old social worker, Stephen, has lived a

sincere life seeking to "fix" others, while sabotaging his own journey through many compulsive, self-destructive choices. He was tortured by his estranged relationship with his father, a man who either neglected him or derogated him without mercy. At last, the father was on his deathbed with emphysema and Stephen went to visit him in one last attempt at connection. "Why did you not like me?" he asks his gasping father, and his father rasps out a list of reasons. The one I remember went something like, "When you were ten, you dropped your toy down the toilet and I had to take it apart to get the toy out." Stephen left his father for the last time, and the man died shortly thereafter. "He gave me the only gift I ever really got from him," Stephen explained. "All this time I thought I was simply not a good son, whatever that is supposed to be. At the end, what he gave me as his only gift was the knowledge that it wasn't me, but that Dad was effing crazy." It seems a small gift, but remember, Stephen had lived his life in service to a "story"—inaccurate yes, but a story in which he was defined as an unworthy child. Many of his subsequent choices were extrapolations of this story. Bringing that implicit story across the threshold of consciousness allowed Stephen to begin making other choices in his life, shuffling off the burden of a damning history. In time, he even gained a measure of forgiveness as he pondered what stories his father unconsciously served, stories that made him so bitter, so condemning of others. Surely, his father must have hated himself, too. Jung observed that the greatest burden a child must bear is the unlived life of the parent, so Stephen's burden was not just living his father's unconscious story, but having to take on the task of redeeming not only his own internalized father complex, but his father's invisible history as well. Freed of that defining story, Stephen is now more able to determine whether his occupation is right for him, or an enslaving assignment to repair someone else's history.

Without a larger measure of consciousness, we cannot begin to struggle with fate. We rather remain its prisoner. It behooves all of us to look at the prevalent patterns of our lives and ask what "story" they might be serving. We do not do crazy things; we do logical things, *if* we understand the "reason" that generates our behaviors. The "reason" may be inaccurate, a misreading of the world, true only for a particular moment and place, or even the inheritance of someone else's story, but, remaining unconscious, it commands sufficient power to govern our story, and therewith dictates the unfolding pattern of our lives.

Consider a woman, Naomi, who lived with a cold and remote mother, and who never met her father. Her clear message internalized from her mother/daughter experience was "You will not receive what you need from her, but you better learn to take care of her because she is the only one you have." In her thirties she forms a partnership with a very narcissistic, abusive woman and finds herself used—sexually, financially, emotionally—but feels powerless in the face of this exploitation. Is her bondage to the past any wonder to us who have a certain remove, an awareness of her primal story and the "instructions" that accompany it? How often do any of us, or all of us, repeat silent "instructions" like these? How long it took Naomi to recognize that her partner was reenacting for her the familiar parent/child script in which she gets next to nothing, the other is sovereign, yet she had better hang on for dear life because that's the only relationship she is going to get. And how humbling it is to any of us when we discover the primitive, archaic origins of our "instructions," and acknowledge for the first time the secret hand of fate.

Or consider Franklin. Surrounded by emotionally undeveloped but manipulative parents, he learned early to finesse others to get what he wanted from them. After internalizing his family's manipulative style, seduction—whether in business or romance—proved easy. He knew what women wanted to hear. He could be soft and sensitive when they wanted that, or in control and decisive when they wanted that. Yet his history of successes with women left him empty, and in his fifties, profoundly alone. The strange ambivalence of his story says to him: "Seduce and manipulate the other for whatever you want, but don't really get close because in the end they will own you." While he has had dozens of relationships, none have lasted because underneath he is terrified of a relationship sticking. What would happen if he were "trapped" by the other, bound either to the insufficiency or domination he had come to expect from others? We can see how this history-laden story plays out in what Freud called "the repetition compulsion," the need to revisit the original dynamics, even when they have predictable, painful conclusions. In Franklin's therapy his recognition of the power of the received story, and the complex it begot,* felt shattering.

---

* Such a complex is often called "the *puer aeternus*," or "the *puella aeternus*" if a woman—namely, "the eternal child." As they once experienced substantive psychological domination from a parent figure, such a person is still governed by the parental imago, and he or she dances about from relationship to relationship, yet is terrified of being captured by the Other. (See Marie-Louise von Franz's *The Problem of the Puer Aeternus* for a full discussion of this complex).

In his conscious life, he sought to live ethically, but he realized how he repetitively manipulates the psyches of others, leaving them, and himself, wounded, bereft, and sterile. Breaking from the power of that story, that fated imposition of a received narrative, demands that we accord fate its power, but also fight its domination.

Or consider Jennell. Daughter of two very driven, narcissistic parents, who demanded that she live out their values, marry the person who met their criteria, and follow the forms that they considered "success," she spent much time weeping in my office, and considered herself a "failure." Why would she reach this conclusion when she was bright, gifted, self-supporting? Well, for starters, her parents continued to undermine her, critique her, and admonish her. They did not like her work; they did not like her husband; they did not like her politics. "Why am I so miserable, such a failure?" she asked in so many ways. She was incredulous when I said that, quite to the contrary, I considered her heroic and successful—very successful. When Jennell asked how that could possibly be the case, I replied that she had to notice that every time she got emotionally ill, from childhood, through adolescence, college, and even now, it was on those occasions when she was following the received "script," enacting someone else's story rather than her own. Notwithstanding, she had made her most important adult choices quite contrary to her parents' wishes, yet neither in a spirit of rebellion nor overcompensation.

Together we concluded that her parents' script was never really about her, but rather in service to making them feel better about the choices they had made. In short, their life-long conflictual relationship was not about loving her for who she was, but in service to their own narcissistically driven efforts to shore up their shaky relationship to the Self.

Jennell was heroic and successful, I told her, because she had, finally, privileged the relationship with her soul over the parental complexes, made different choices and thereby created a different story. Naturally, she carried within her the archaic need to please her parents, in return for which they would love her, protect her, approve of her, but such a profound, understandable need was no longer autonomously making choices for her. She was "successful" because she was risking her talents, her emotional life, and her own sociopolitical values; in short, she had become a grown-up, and in our banal and trivializing time, that is quite an accomplishment. No matter how ambushed she still is on a daily basis by those archaic messages, she is steadily forging her way, finding her path through the various snares that fate has set for her. That is why she is heroic.

FIGHTING FATE, LOVING FATE

The point has been made by now, I trust, that our story can be changed—with consciousness, risk, courage, investment of energy, and persistence. A sustained therapy identifying what stories have been internalized, how they repetitiously impose the past upon the present, and how we may convert the directives of history into a larger frame of possibility is but one avenue of liberation. I have frequently asserted that the real goal of a depth therapy is not a "cure," for the human condition is not a disease. Yes, real, resistant problems of daily life can and must be addressed and the resources of consciousness and intentionality brought fully to bear on their resolution. But the real gift of a depth therapy, or any truly conscious, considered life, is that one achieves a deepened conversation around the meaning of one's journey—a conversation without which one lives a received life, not one's own, a superficial life, or a life in service to complexes and ideologies. But what of those parts of the story that cannot be changed, that resist our denials, our distractions, our sincere, best efforts? Perhaps then we have also to recover a sense of what our ancestors paradoxically called *amor fati*, the love of one's fate.

How can one fight one's fate, force an aperture into larger life, and yet still *love* one's fate, especially the limiting, painful parts of it? This issue is, of course, one of the oldest of philosophical conundrums—the contention between freedom and determination. Frankly, the older I get, the more I see patterns in my own life, as well as patterns playing out in the lives of analysands, and am reluctantly forced to conclude that we are far less free than we believe. Further, I have come to consider most of what passes for "self-help" literature today as obscene because it ignores the complexities of life, glosses over the ardor and commitment required for change, and promises panaceas not likely to happen. These banal insults to the depth of our souls will almost always end with disappointment, disillusionment, or further self-castigation, for they ignore the immense power of fate, which is to say, the sovereignty of the gods. Add to that the humbling reminder that the unconscious *is* unconscious, and we are compelled to respect even more the powerful currents that sweep us across a vast, tenebrous sea.

What is most deceptive to ego consciousness is that the psyche is a shape-shifter, a protean puzzle outwardly changing appearances, but with an invisible constancy of dynamic patterns underneath. Similarly, the old sea-god Proteus forever deceives—each wave is different, fragile and frangible, but the sea still serves the eternal laws of ebb, flow, and mathematic progressions.

Despite my growing awareness of the determinative powers that infiltrate our lives, I have spent my personal and professional life devoted to teaching and therapy as empowering agencies that wedge out narrow apertures into larger possibilities, while admitting privately that perhaps the cruelest determinism might be found in this seductive fantasy of freedom. Notwithstanding, as Jean-Paul Sartre once expressed it, in what concrete situations do we act *as if* we are free? Acting through the fantasy of freedom, in existential rebellion, is not only the source of our dignity, moral choice, and responsibility, but also the ineluctable fundament of our values, lest we be nothing more than passive playthings of an indifferent universe or capricious gods. In the end, we may not "love" our fate, but we can love the life we wrested from the grip of fate.

THE DEBT WE OWE TO FATE

If we are free, as free as we want to think we are, then our lives should rather easily take care of themselves. We would make appropriate, proactive choices, and life would work out pretty much as we consciously plan. Surely any reader of this book is mature enough to see beyond that fantasy by now. What, after all, has brought us to these sundry impasses, these stuck points in our lives? And who is responsible if not us? Clearly there are other agencies at work in our lives at all times, often with wills and agendas contrary to our intentions or desires. As you know, our ancestors called these agencies "the gods," or, variously, labeled the negative outcomes of our choices as *sin*, or presumptive offenses of "the gods." *The gods* then are those archetypal force fields in which we swim, yet that transcend our conscious life and exceed our personal powers. Thus, the tragic vision, or variously, the drama of sin, punishment, and possible redemption, is the story of coming back to right relationship with these imperial powers.

One of the ways in which humans have historically accommodated, if not rationalized, the weighty influences of fate upon our lives is with the idea of *karma*. (The word tracks back to what was once honored as the triple goddess *Car* who incarnated as maiden, mother, and crone, the troika that governs time and presides over outcomes. From her multiple ministries, all events flow, including our "freest of choices.") Acknowledging the powers of determinism, and accepting the unacceptable, namely that we have no choice, really, no alternative, is to assert that we serve and beget new karma—the accumulation of history, the detritus of consequences. Serving the assignment this life brings us well, faithfully, and affirmatively can remove some small portion of the cumulative weight of history and free the soul for the next round of the bout with karma. In time, with sufficient acceptance, repentance, and faithful conduct, one might at last escape the iron bonds of history and achieve nirvana, the freedom of nothingness. Meanwhile, this ego, and what we consider this current life, is never more than a wafer bobbing in the vast inner sea of the unconscious, and upon a much larger milky sea of the cosmos.

Perhaps the most insidious of such karmic messages in our time and place is that we say to the child, "You must be successful, affluent, powerful, married to the right person," and so on. Each child is thus launched in service to the parent's neurosis, and gets further and further from his or her own soul. Or, as earlier identified, the motif of "the wounded healer" is another illustration of how a child's own healthy strivings can be warped by the defining norms of family environment with its sundry messages. Foremost among those messages is the implicit admonition: "You are not here to live your life, but to repair the broken journeys of those around you. Perhaps then, perhaps . . . you may get to your life at last." So, in response to the power of the explicit and implicit messages, children spend their lives repeating the message, over and over, running from it but backing into it again, or trying to fix it through drugs, distraction, or passing it on to their children. Jung once observed that "behind the wound lies the genius" of the person, for there is where his or her energies will be invested, adaptations most skillful, and attitudes toward self and world most fixed. Much good has come from those who are trying to fix the wounds of the world, but how free, then, are they, and what would they have done with their lives if they had truly been free to serve the soul that is great within all of us?

Additionally, the more we learn from genetics, brain chemistry, the sociobiologists, the more we learn that our lives are driven by inherited forces. Our word *fate* comes from the Latin *fatum*, meaning "to speak." Thus, it would seem, *the gods have spoken*, and that is an end to that. We recall that the classical imagination personified three specific Fates: *Lachesis*, who grants a particular lot to each of us;

Clotho, who reiterates, ratifies these givens; and the spinner *Atropos*, who weaves the web of cause and effect and nets us in inevitabilities. Add to that the structural elements that limit all things by internal laws, personified as *Ananke*, or impersonal "necessity," whereby, for example, all rising things fall at last to earth, and life seems pretty much a done deal. Indeed, those who would throw up their hands in the face of fate have at least consistency on their side, although Emerson noted that a foolish consistency is the hobgoblin of little minds.

Added to this mix of elements is something unique to each of us called *kharakter*, which is derived from a marking instrument. Thus, there are elements with which we are marked, engraved. Though character can be formed, and modified, we all have inherent tendencies. The truism that sports builds character is of course a lie; rather, as sportswriter Heywood Hale Broun suggested, "it reveals character." None of us would admit to having "bad character," although we have all done bad things. In fact, a person who has never done anything "bad" will be a pretty superficial, infantile being, and that is a bad thing.

So is any one of us happy with our fate? Do we not all possess infinite desires, but finite capacities? Have we just packed this question away in the attic like yesterday's fashions? What do we owe to fate, and what to the possibility of freedom, then? Therein are the real questions.

Put most succinctly, having been given life, what we now owe fate is two things, a life fully lived, and our death in return. However much the nervous ego or the neurotic culture wishes otherwise, *we all owe life a death. In fact, perhaps we owe life many of them.* Many revere Buddha, for example, because he was able to die unto this life, or Jesus because he could say, "not my will but Thine," and, even more, "Unless ye die, ye shall not live." Both of these cultural paradigms personified a path of individuation: not that we are to live their lives—they did that already—but that we are to surrender to what calls us forth most deeply into life and into death. For example, many times in the context of therapy I have said, in the face of painful, limiting blows that a person has suffered, that "the meaning of your life from this point on will be the degree to which you can express yourself more fully in the face of this situation." As the only true pathology is denial, we cannot run from fate by denying its wounding impact. But we can work with it, and even occasionally triumph in the face of its limitations.

I can think of many examples—among them is a woman who has expressed her sorrow that no one ever loved her. Her task is thus to find forms of self-love, despite a history of bad choices in service to this message of unworthiness. Learning that her dreams spoke to her from a place transcendent to consciousness led in time to a greater trust in the generative Self than in the many complexes generated by her biography. Time after time her dream life presented her with "children" whom she was to take into her care. It was unthinkable that she would leave these deserving, vulnerable children to fend for themselves. Can we not see in this repetitive imagery that something larger than ego, larger than complexes, "loves" her, and asks her active participation in healing? She came to see and trust that possibility and, while her present life is not without sorrow, it is richer and more empowered than ever.

Or another man, who was driven by the need for competitive success, power, and money, fell at last to his knees

and recognized that his womanizing and drug use had anes-
thetized the pain of his inner life for so many years. He is
now sober, in a committed relationship, and in love with his
life for the first time.

These examples can be repeated by the thousands as we
struggle to live meaningfully in contexts over which we have
no control.

Perhaps the ancients were right about Fate, perhaps the
emerging, deterministic scientific reports are right—perhaps
we are bound to the iron wheel of *Samsara**—but we are still
here to live our lives to the fullest. Tipping our hat to Fate, acknowledging that the gods choose the playing field upon which
we find ourselves, we are still here to play the game. The object
is not to win or lose, for that is already decided, and already
irrelevant**—for us it is rather to be on the playing field, with
utmost exercise of élan and investment of spirit to the end.

Albert Camus wrestled with this paradox in his reworking
of the myth of Sisyphus. As we recall, Sisyphus, having offended the gods, is obliged to roll a boulder up a hill, perpetually, and then to watch it roll back down the hill, perpetually.
Given our modernist fantasy of *progress*, this image of cosmic
futility is quite offensive to us. We think of ourselves as a
can-do culture, but we continue to mess up in the same old
ways that the parables and tragedies of our ancestors illus-
trated so powerfully for us.*** Yet Camus imagines that he can

---

* *Samsara* is the Sanskrit word for the endlessly revolving wheel of reincarnation.

** Or, as Damon Runyon once put it, "Life is eight to five . . . against."

*** Illustrations of these historic repetitions proliferate, though what we can learn
from them continues to be lost on most of us. Inevitably, how arrogance and
ignorance collude in overreaching, setting up reactionary consequences, and
ending in decline, is playing out on both national and personal levels as I
write.

see the face of Sisyphus at the bottom of the hill, facing the futile task once again, and, wait . . . is that a smile that plays across his face? Yes, in smiling, Sisyphus *chooses* to push the boulder back up the hill, and therein wrests from the gods his freedom. A pragmatist might argue, "Hey, same hill, same boulder, same outcome." But life is more than outcomes; it is also attitude.

Similarly, psychiatrist Viktor Frankl described how the Holocaust took his family, his work, his home, and his freedom from him, in fact took everything but what he found to be his "final freedom," namely, the power to choose his attitude toward the circumstances in which he found himself and over which he had no control. Imprisoned as he was by thugs, he remained the custodian of his soul, the arbiter of his ethics. Whether he sustained a private, inner freedom and rebellion, whether he preserved the flickering flame of spirit and of conscience, whether he added to the healing of the suffering community around him, was still his choice. Later in life, Frankl developed what he called "logotherapy," the therapy of meaning, for he concluded that we can live with multiple wounds of fate, but cannot live without meaning. Similarly, Jung observed that our neuroses are forms of suffering that have not yet found their meaning. Either way, suffering is part of our condition, but life may either be enlarged or diminished by our choices. Likewise, theologian Dietrich Bonhoeffer smuggled out a letter from a concentration camp just before his execution. In it he asked if that terrible place in which he was thrust, Flossenbürg concentration camp, was created by the will of God. He concluded it was not, that those impoverished precincts of perversity were created by humans who arrogated the power over life or death to themselves. Yet his spiritual task remained, namely, to work *through* these awful conditions to find the will of God for him there. In these, and so many other ways, we pay our dues to fate, live in full acknowledgment of its obdurate powers, and may still exercise our existential revolt in search of meaning. Meaning is found both through the acceptance of fate *and* in the struggle to remain free, to make value choices amid a constricted range of possibilities. Whatever the gods do, we are still summoned to continue to be the guardians of our souls.

All of the great religious traditions convey this profound paradox, expressed more directly as submission to the will of God. The word *Islam* means to submit or surrender to the deity, Allah. Jewish and Christian wisdom traditions urge surrender to the will of God, and we recall Dante's "*in la sua voluntade e nostra pace,*" "in Thy will is our peace." We also know that whatever the mystery of healing is, it requires surrender to a higher will—the will of the body, the flow of *ki*, or *shi*, or *chi*, and the overcoming of the complex-driven ego's obsessive fantasy of sovereignty. All of the Twelve Step groups begin with the challenge to accept one's worst nightmare, namely, that one is really not in charge after all. Only after confessing the bankruptcy of one's compulsive treatment plan may healing begin.

Paradoxically, this "surrender" is the critical step in recovering our paths, resuming the Dharma road toward personhood. However imbued or constricted with developmental possibilities our destiny may be, our calling is necessarily played out upon the field and within the forms granted us by the gods. Stepping up to this task is the greatest affirmation we can bring to our journey.

While the chief agenda of the first half of life is to develop an ego, a sense of self strong enough to leave parents, step out into the world, and create a provisional life, the agenda of the second half surely asks us to reconsider: Now, in service to what do I live my life? Much of the second half of life is fueled by the need for meaning. We have charged up hills, achieved results of one kind or another, suffered collateral damage to ourselves and others, and are then brought to our knees and forced to ask, "Where do I go from here, and for what reasons?" While the first half of life may be said to be a series of responses to and internalizations of the messages our fated environment presents us, the second half of life requires a recovery of personal authority, if we are ever to live our lives and not someone else's.

Another way in which we live honestly with this paradox is to remember the admonition of our ancestors, who, in so many ways and in so many traditions, reminded us, "Neither too high, nor too low." The more we identify with Fate, the more depressed and bound we feel; the more we identify with freedom, the less we are likely to look for the invisible hand of Fate in our lives. As Emerson reminds us, "Always pay; for first or last you must pay your entire debt. Persons and events may stand for a time between you and justice, but it is only a postponement. You must pay at last your own debt."*

So much of our lives has been given to us, for good or ill—parental environment, culture, biology, and the like—and we can spend all our time kvetching and wishing it were otherwise, but as we all know, such whining is just a waste. I have sometimes seen women understandably agitated by

---

* Emerson, *The Writings of Ralph Waldo Emerson*, p. 181.

their husbands' departure who nevertheless spend the rest of their lives blaming; when, if at all, did they pull up their own socks and get on with their life? Often, they are most angry because they gave over their individuation imperative to him and now are enraged that they are asked to accept that responsibility for themselves. And I have seen men complaining that their partners do not understand them. Yes, it is true that we never really understand each other, even after many years of sincere effort. But those men wish someone else to understand the depth and purpose of their souls when they have barely begun to take on that daunting project for themselves. It is much easier to project the anima onto another woman than to admit that one is the custodian of one's own soul first, long before it can be shared with another.

Anyone conscious of, or reflective upon, his or her history will be humbled and obliged to pause and discern those threads of influence that are at work in us all the while. I certainly never expected to be in the roles that I enact today. But as I reflect on them, I find they are all in service to the same questions I had as a child. To put it in archetypal metaphor, I have come to realize that I am now and have always been in service to the god *Hermes*.* While himself a god, Hermes was also a messenger of the gods; he was a god of "in-betweens." As a therapist, a writer, a teacher, I spend my life pondering the obscure messages of the gods. In the congress and concourse of daily life, I move between the mysteries of divinity and the symptomatological expressions of

---

* *Hermeneutics* is the discipline of interpretation, expanded today from the elucidation of sacred texts by our recognition that the sacred courses beneath the surface of the secular as well. *Mercury* is his Latin name, and he appears as the logo for Western Union, a conveyor of messages.

patients, the elucidation of texts, and the shifting nexuses between people. Interpreting, clarifying, being led to new levels of mystery is service to Hermes—it is the thread that unites all the areas of my life, and the directive energy that thrums beneath the surface of my biography. All of us need to reflect upon what "gods" are at work within us, what their energies ask of us, and to submit our serviceable egos to their agendas, which often transcend our desires for pleasure, security, satiety, and consensual validation.

This "heroic submission" is what we owe Fate, the gods, and our own soul. This is both existential revolt and *amor fati*. Loving one's Fate means that we live as fully as we can the life to which the gods have summoned us. We are not here to imitate those who have gone before, for that was *their* life, someone else's journey. We are here to figure out and serve what life asks of *us.* This is not resignation, it is not defeat, it is not fatalism, it is not passivity, it is oxymoronically "heroic submission," for the hero archetype is called to serve life, not the ego. The heroic task is found wherever we overcome fear and lethargy, wherever we embrace the larger, wherever our timorous agenda is defeated by ever larger things. In the midst of defeat for the ego, we are blessed with concomitant abundance. As young people, we are not yet ready to live this defeat, for we are convinced of the powers of will and all that it can bring us. And we need to live that will out, until we come to our accounting, to our place in the wilderness where strange paths fork off into that tangled grove where the gods live.

We have to earn the capacity to surrender, for it takes much living, and a lot of difficult times, before any of us has the right to claim what Yeats wrote toward the end of his days as he reviewed his life story. Ailing in spirit and bone, chastened by life and its disappointments, he winds his way through to a place to which we might all aspire, to the love of one's fate.

> I am content to follow to its source
> Every event in action or in thought;
> Measure the lot; forgive myself the lot!
> When such as I cast out remorse
> So great a sweetness flows into the breast
> We must laugh and we must sing,
> We are blest by everything,
> Everything we look upon is blest.*

* W. B. Yeats, "A Dialogue of Self and Soul," in *Selected Poems and Two Plays*, p. 125.

Chapter Twelve

THAT WE LIVE MORE FULLY IN THE SHADOW OF MORTALITY

". . . nature's bonfire burns on.
But quench her bonniest, dearest to her, her clearest-selved spark
Man, how fast his firedint, his mark on mind, is gone!

G. M. HOPKINS, "THAT NATURE IS A HERACLITEAN FIRE"

"The universe is a fleeting idea in God's mind . . . a pretty
uncomfortable thought if you've just made a down payment on
a house."

WOODY ALLEN

"This spectacle of old age would be unendurable did we not know
that our psyche reaches into a region held captive neither by
change in time nor by limitation of place. In that form of being our
birth is a death and our death a birth. The scales of the whole
hang balanced."

C. G. JUNG

*T*he greatest, perduring affront to sovereign fantasies of
the human ego is its perishability—the fact of which is profoundly inscribed in and unfolding through the eschatology of
our cells during each moment of this querulous, quarrelsome

journey. All rising things fall; all ascendant things return to earth; all bodies in motion submit to the law of inertia. The pragmatic question that confronts us, then, is *what does this fact make us do*, or *keep us from doing*? And how might we live more *abundantly* in the presence of our mortality? And, finally, does mortality even matter? The core idea in this chapter is that an aroused awareness of mortality is not the same as fear of mortality. Daily we are summoned to be mindful of mortality in order not to tumble into triviality, or be unconsciously governed by fear of that which is our most natural fact.

Understandably, the quickened consciousness of what German philosopher Martin Heidegger called the *Being-towards-death*—that is, us—is always founded in the fact that our deep ground and ineluctable direction leads to annihilation. Of the profuse examples of this preoccupation, I first think on the lyric of the seventeenth-century poet Thomas Nashe, in his "A Litany in Time of Plague."

> *Fond are life's lustful joys;*
> *Death proves them all but toys;*
> *None from his darts can fly;*
> *I am sick, I must die.*
> *Lord have mercy on us!**

Nashe was writing in the time of the plague, when death was all around him, against which the plaints of persons and powers were equally futile. Sacred and secular institu-

---

* Thomas Nashe, "A Litany in Time of Plague," *The Norton Anthology of Poetry*, p. 202.

tion alike failed to stem the terrible tumbrels filled with corpses, and the most compassionate, those who stayed to help their comrades, died faster than those who fled. And today, for all our delusions of sovereignty, amid the stunning prolongation of the human life span, I write in a time when death is all around us also, whether in metastatic cell, foreign adventure, bursting vessel, violence in the marketplace, or simply a failure to waken one morning. All of our instrumentalities, our wondrous medical armamentaria, only extend our stay against annihilation a few years at best. Our fear of annihilation leads, as we know, to denial, displacement, distraction, projection, frantic efforts to transcend the condition, and various numbing strategies. As that contemporary theologian Woody Allen once observed, "The lion shall lie down with the lamb, but the lamb won't get very much sleep."

We are living longer and longer as a species, but in service to what? Andrew Achenbaum presents these tantalizing facts:

At the time of the American Revolution, the median age of Americans was sixteen;

At the time of our Civil War, half the population was under age twenty;

As late as 1950, only half the population was over thirty;

Currently, the number of men and women over sixty-five has increased by 1,100 percent, and the number of centenarians has doubled since 1980.*

---

* Andrew Achenbaum, *Older Americans, Vital Communities: A Bold Vision for Societal Aging*, p. 1.

214 · JAMES HOLLIS, PH.D.

Since so many of us are living so much longer, may we inquire if longevity itself is the goal, or is it something else? Are our lives four times richer, more meaningful, than those who lived in ancient Greece, or twice richer, more meaningful, than those who lived just a century ago? Will those who live longer into this present century live better lives, and how would we know that? How do we define "better"—by "longevity"? Finally . . . finally, why *should* we live longer—just because our neuroses say so? And does the universe agree with our conclusions? Freud was heroic when it came to this question. While in the terminal phase of his cancer of the jaw, having no belief in an afterlife, he observed that his removal from life would have minimal consequence because he had contributed the piece of the puzzle he knew and believed, and had nothing further to say.* He was, it would seem, able to accept his end with equanimity, courage, and finality.

As we know, extensive industries thrive on our fear of aging, infirmity, and death. The increase of surgeries to present a contrived appearance to the world is evident. We use the phrase "heroic measures" to describe our combat with death, as if death were an "enemy" rather than the natural order of things—regardless of whether one considers the natural order to be merely "nature naturing" or the acts and will of a superordinate divinity. We say sixty is the new fifty, and so on. While there is nothing at all wrong about celebrating life and health, what lies beneath so much of this

---

* But in the face of this heroic acceptance, Freud was moved by U.S. Ambassador Bullock to write a short piece on Woodrow Wilson, of all people, a president who in his narrow but inflated state believed that he spoke for Divinity, had a large but naive vision of world order, and refused to accept contradictory advice. Like other inflated chief executives, this benighted soul created ripples in history that continued to roll back on his nation's shores for decades to come.

hoorah is the disruptive specter of death. More exercise, more vitamins, more surgery, and we will soon live forever, or at least much longer, extending tomorrow indefinitely. The Greeks had a story about this: Tithonus, who was immortal but who grew to hate his life because his choices had ceased to matter. He could choose this path for this century, and then casually another for the next, and thus the years stretched meaninglessly through tendentious permutations of time. Finally, he petitioned the gods for release from eternity to become mortal *so that his choices might matter*, that whatever he chose might actually count for something. The gods blessed him by granting his wish.

This ancient story still resonates for us. How is it that a person might achieve what he or she wants in this life and still feel miserable? Is that not the story of so much of modern Western culture, where attaining material comforts unthinkable to our predecessors has led not to contentment but rather to ennui, neuroses, and social disorders? Tithonus achieved our presumptive goal—immortality—and ultimately disdained its gift. It is troubling to consider that we, too, might find that what we want—that is, what the timorous ego under the influence of a complex may want—may not be in our interest in the bigger picture. (And, remember, this story is over two and a half millennia old.)

But just to see how timeless this dilemma is, let us go back even earlier, to c. 2750 B.C.E., a thousand years before the *Iliad* and the Bible. Written in the cradle of Western civilization,* Iraq, *Gilgamesh* similarly dramatizes a story

---

* The tablets were found in a place now named Mosul, Iraq, a geo-nexus so pivotal that its spilled blood still appears on our newscasts.

that echoes perpetually through the halls of *archeology*,* a discipline whose etymology reveals the resonant persistence of an archaic, wordless word.

Gilgamesh is a great hero, part god, part human, who initially embodies anarchic libido and crude power over others. But over time that power is tempered, civilized, humanized, both in his encounter with the "feminine" embodied in a temple prostitute through whom he learns relatedness, and an engagement with his shadow through his friendship with comrade Enkidu. Later, grieving his lost friend, and with his own death approaching, Gilgamesh is anxiously driven to find immortality. Frustrated in this goal, he asks what matters in the end. The response, all those millennia ago—and a thousand years before the quite similar advice of Ecclesiastes—is that he must faithfully attend the tasks of daily life, love those who are part of his world, and submit to the will of the gods. This testimony from ancient Iraq reminds us that, for all our differences of outer cultural forms, all who have preceded us have had the identical issues that we do: to claim selfhood, to find and nurture relationship, to work creatively within the limits of a contingent world, and to live more fully in the shadow of death.

❖ ❖ ❖

Is not all of this earnest effort, all this evasion, all this preoccupation with annihilation at bottom an ego problem? We do have, and need, an ego, for what it provides is a clustered

---

* *Arché* (ancient, primal) + *logos* (word, expression). As Gerhard Hauptmann described, we hear archaic "echoes of the wordless word" in the myths of our predecessors.

energy necessary for the tasks of consciousness: intentionality, consistency of purpose, ethical choice. Still, was not Freud dead-on when he stepped outside his ego, and, like Gautama, saw through the delusions under which the ego may be enslaved by one complex or another? Why should *I* live longer? Should *I* live longer than my ancestors? Should *I* live longer than you, the reader? Should *I* outlast my children, a horror that I have seen, with great sadness, afflict some really good folks and tarnish their days forever?* Should I simply "grow up" and accept the fact that the next knock on the door may be the Big Guy with the scythe and shroud? And will I be able to say, as I do hope, when he does show: "Well, now it's my turn. Much better folks than *moi* have not lived so long, nor been so privileged as I."** I do believe, and do hope I will so affirm. But I may still have an "attytood"*** about it.

Humankind has forever posited the idea of an afterlife. If there is an afterlife, then it is *another* life than this one. Meanwhile, we are *here*, with this one . . . for the moment at least. The truth is, no one knows, no matter what they say, and with what neurotic fervor they say it. Intuitively, it makes sense that this energy system does not go "away," but it sure does go somewhere. And would our ego consciousness still

---

* Among the many examples, I think first of the books by my colleagues Charlotte Mathes, *And a Sword Shall Pierce Your Heart,* and M. J. Hurley Brant, *When Every Day Matters.*

** I hope this does not sound gratuitous, but I really do measure my safe longevity against the reality of those children put on cattle cars to Auschwitz. While I, their contemporary, was protected thousands of miles away, they were sent to slaughter by stunted bigots simply for having been born who and where they were.

*** Translated, this is, of course, Phillyspeak for *attitude.*

be around to know it, appreciate the fact, wherever it might be? I recall an elderly lady in my neighborhood who spoke to me, a child then, of her imminent plans for walking the golden streets of Heaven. Not fully up on metaphor in those early days, I wondered whether those streets were really hard metal. But I did not doubt her belief. And I do hope she is there, dear sweet soul that she was, and has also found a place to rest her tired feet. And, ratiocination aside, I do also hope to reunite with lost loved ones.

The persistent idea of the *soul* posits something nonmaterial, transcendent to the body. When this mortal coil is shuffled off, to use the imagery of brother Hamlet, will we be floating spirits somewhere, disembodied, or will we have our bodies? What stage of development might we recover—the infant crawling or the aged—both with halting steps? (Or is that literalizing a metaphor too much?) And, as my mother-in-law poignantly wondered after multiple amputations, would her limbs be restored in that place? Again, I do hope so for her. And some days, against all reason, as I confessed above, I still expect to see my Shadrach again—our beloved Lhasa who regularly appears in my dreams, and to whom I speak every day as I round a certain curve on the way to work.

Many people of faith accept the assurances of their founders, or their leaders, and proclaim the promises of Jesus or Mohammed and others. Others expect nihilation. Still others have suggested that we get precisely the afterlife we imagined. Sartre worried that the afterlife might be a hell of other people; Woody Allen suggested that it might be a small room where an insurance salesman will read the *entire* policy to you through the centuries; poet Billy Collins speculated that some of us would find Edith Hamilton and her mad, three-headed dog on the scene if we were classicists, or, if we were merely jaded moderns, a room with a noisy air conditioner and babbling chorus girls; other poets, like Wallace Stevens and Stephen Dunn,* have repeatedly asserted that they have learned to foreswear shaky promises and live more fully in *this* fallen, precious, richly divine world.

Still others, as in Judaism, have posited the idea that one lives through one's descendants, which is certainly true to some degree, if only genetically. But is it not likely that by the third or fourth generation this generation will be pretty much forgotten anyway? As you may recall Shakespeare's 154 sonnets, mostly written at the time of the closing of London's theaters in the 1590s because of the plague, have essentially one theme, namely, "You and I will die, but these verses will not, and therefore you and I live onward through these lines." Thus, with the charnel houses filling, the passing bell an hourly sound, and the dead trundled in tumbrels to dumping grounds, Shakespeare quelled his terror with the thought of literary immortality. A modern, Archibald MacLeish, specifically challenges this Elizabethan fantasy in a poem that says to the beloved, in so many words: "Look, you and I are going to die; the readers of this poem will die; the page will turn to dust, so I won't delude ourselves into immortal pretensions, but rather I will say, simply, *I saw you there*, outlined in the doorway, with the sun at your back—*I saw you*."** That is the best love poem I

---

* Cf. for example, Wallace Stevens's "Sunday Morning," and Stephen Dunn's "A Postmortem Guide."

** Cf. Archibald MacLeish's "Not Marble Nor the Gilded Monuments."

ever read, and the most honest I have ever found about this whole business.*

But the truth is, we do not know. As brother Hamlet asserts, that "undiscovered country, from whose borne no traveler has returned,"** provides scant credible data—at least none whose testimony we can credit with the modern intelligence you or I might bring to the table. Similarly, as novelist E. M. Forster noted, those two characters who might best inform us about whence and whither, the infant and the corpse, are notoriously silent on the matter also. We also recall the five stages of dying articulated by Kübler-Ross—denial, anger, bargaining, depression, acceptance . . . when or if acceptance happens. (I recall my mother, dying of esophageal and stomach cancer, asking me to reiterate these five stages, which I did. "At least," she said, "I am not in denial.")

So, where does all this leave us, if we wish to be intellectually honest, emotionally mature, and yet more than merely implicated, more or less involved, in this conundrum? As Jung wisely noted:

> People who most feared life when they were young . . .
> suffer later just as much from the fear of death. When they
> are young one says they have infantile resistances against
> the normal demands of life; one should really say the same
> thing when they are old, for they are likewise afraid of
> one of life's normal demands. We are so convinced that

---

* A possible rival to this claim is Charles Baudelaire's poem "A Carcass," in which the speaker notes a splayed rotting carcass of a cow on the roadside, with its black flags of swarming flies, and reminds his beloved that she will someday look that way as well. Such romantics the French are!

** *Hamlet*, Act III, Sc. 1.

death is simply the end of a process that it does not ordinarily occur to us to conceive of death as a goal and a fulfillment, as we do without hesitation the aims and purposes of your life in its ascendance.*

Jung's acknowledgment of our splitting from the life force and its ineluctable agenda compels us to revisit this issue. While the ego reiterates its defensive "attytood," our very unfolding nature posits another. Whipsawed by two such compelling realities, no wonder we grow neurotic, and are prey to the most abysmal fears, escapist fantasies, and cheap distractions.

One thing I have observed directly and many, many times as an analyst is that those who feel that they have taken risks, who, generally speaking, have lived their lives, have a much better time with their dying. None of us is able to jam it all in, or make all the "right" choices; moreover, even the "right" choices might have produced other unforeseen consequences. But it is clear that those who fail to risk being who they are, who shun diving into the journey, are the most fear-ridden, regretful, and recriminating. With such a compromised purchase on their own history, they blame others, castigate themselves, or live with debilitating regrets. This is a bad way to go.

Paradoxically, it is our mortality that gives us meaning, as Tithonus learned. Mortality means that our choices really do matter. Did not the learned Dr. Samuel Johnson observe that there is nothing that quickens the sensibility more sharply than the threat of the noose? At those moments we

---

* Jung, "The Soul and Death," *The Structure and Dynamics of the Psyche*, CW 8, par. 797.

realize that we live a very short, intense time. When viewed from the prospect of eternity, are we really much more durable than the fireflies?

> The firefly light pattern is a mating signal. Males blink a certain sequence and hope to see an answering flash from a female. Each of the 200 species have their own signal. . . . Fireflies live for two years as larvae, eating worms from the soil, and for just two weeks as adults—enjoying just 14 nights of flying, flashing and courtship, then it is all over. For them, it is a very short, intense time.*

Well . . . great and abiding thanks to those intrepid scientists who solved this mystery for us! Never mind why we might, in a "projective identification," use the word *enjoyed* to describe their fourteen nights, or why we might be interested, except that we *are* interested, and are implicated. For we are the neurotic beasts, what Nietzsche called "the sick animal"—cursed with consciousness, morbid reflection, and the capacity to anticipate—all of which are necessary ingredients for existential angst. For us, it is a very short, intense time also, and amid whatever distracting flying and flashing we manage, we know it most of the way. Such a brief visit asks of us courage and reasonable dignity, and yet so frequently we fall prey to delusion, denial, and depression.

One of our most heroic models is described in Plato's account of the final hours of Socrates. Judged democratically but prejudicially on spurious charges, the Sage of Athens is

---

* Paul Recer, "Scientists Solve Firefly Mystery." *The Associated Press*, June 28, 2001.

sentenced to execution. His disciples urge him to flee, especially in this case of an apparent miscarriage of justice. But he, loyal citizen of his city-state, abides by the law and its sentence, and willingly takes the draught of hemlock. When asked about death, Socrates opines that either it is the Big Sleep, in which case he can use the rest, or there is an afterlife and he looks forward to conversing with the philosophers who have gone before him. Moreover, he is drawn to the journey toward death because the reflective soul is always summoned to mystery, and to the enlargement that comes from respecting it, considering it, submitting to it. In the end, the life and death of Socrates is a paradigm for all of us; his life and his values constitute a seamless web connecting mysteries of beginning, end, and the profound transformations each brings. Lived with depth, dignity, and passion, his example still means something to us, less perhaps for his philosophical conclusions than his model of a life lived with curiosity and integrity.

WHERE PSYCHE AND SOUL CONVERGE

So what abides, if anything? What persists? What provides continuity, if anything? In considering this issue perhaps we need to return to basics. What is *psyche*? On the literal level *psyche* is the Greek word for *soul*. (Its two etymological roots are the verb "to breathe," *psychein*, and "the butterfly," the former intimating the invisible life force that blows through matter and animates* it. The latter that suggests transformation from the dross to the mysteriously beautiful but elusive.)

---

* Note that the word *animate* contains *anima*, the Latin word for *soul*. So, reportedly, even the material beast we are is en-souled matter, en-souled animal.

Recall that the material form of the book you read, the hand that holds it, the mind that contemplates it, is all in flux, a verb, not a noun.* So what abides, what keeps watch, what provides continuity? *Psyche.*

So we have to explore further the relationship of ego to psyche. To put the matter on the table bluntly: *Whatever we think, feel, believe, hope, from a limited ego frame, is literally irrelevant to the mystery of mortality itself. In death, either the ego is radically transformed in ways we cannot even imagine, or it is annihilated.* Either way, our opinions have the metaphysical ballast of that only—opinions. Again, if there is an afterlife, then it is a life other than the ego images; if there is only annihilation, then we are comrades to the fireflies—with dubious collateral attributes of self-reflection and attendant angst.

In the face of this humiliating affront to ego inflation, we indulge not only in denial and distraction, but excessive nostalgia. Recalling that the etymology of *nostalgia* means a "pain for home," we notice how the ego clings to the past, even the miserable past, because it fears change and development. This attitude is our chief obstacle to an enlarging engagement with the mystery of life and death. We are challenged to live forward—toward and through the many deaths that meet us on a daily basis. Throughout our history, every growth, every change of developmental significance, has been accompanied by a loss of some kind, a price to be paid for the next step of the journey. Whether it was learning to cross the street on our own, learning to take care of ourselves when no one else would, or at this moment learning to

---

* Even Beethoven, reportedly, lies in his grave . . . decomposing.

stand honestly before loss and death, we grow, paradoxically, by losing something. Once again, the price of gain is the loss of something else; the dialectic of growth is always a death of something to which we cling. Of course we wish to honor the past, whether friends, family, or old homes, but an over-attachment to them can be a seductive sleight-of-hand whereby we avoid the next stage of our journey. I know that this all sounds overly rational. But I am not quite a fool, or at least not wholly one. There is real emotion, real cost attendant upon growth and its necessary losses, but excessive attachment is the enemy of the life force itself.

Jung spoke eloquently to the subject of the psychology of the second half of life. On one occasion he concluded:

> We have no schools for forty year olds. . . . Our religions were always such schools in the past, but how many people regard them like that today? . . . A human being would certainly not grow to be seventy or eighty years old if this longevity had no meaning for the species. . . . Whoever carries over into the afternoon the law of the morning . . . must pay for it with damage to his soul.*

Well, so much for nostalgia.

Notice the implications of Jung's remarks. We have to live our lives more reflectively, more responsibly, whether or not there is an afterlife. I would certainly like to believe there is, since I have an ego consciousness, but I also have to live as if there is not. This is not an argument for a depressive attitude

---

* Jung, "The Stages of Life," *The Structure and Dynamics of the Psyche, CW 8,* pars. 786ff.

toward life, or a carpe diem license for excess. It is an argument for considered reflection on the matter. A colleague of mine who worked specifically with the terminally ill said that about one third of them fell into a depression that eroded and contaminated the rest of their lives; about one third sought, in his words, to dance all night; and one third saw it as a time for reflection, change, and enlargement, rather than diminishment. The last words of the novelist Henry James are reported to be, as death approached, "Ah . . . the distinguished thing." If he did not utter these words, they are Jamesian for sure, and he sustained his own authorship up to the end.

Jung's observations suggest not only that nature or divinity might have a purpose for us beyond mere reproduction of the species, and all the frenzied fire-flying of the first half, but that we are summoned to a different psychology by the gift of a so-called second half.* With a mature engagement with the mystery that our mortality demands, we may find that our goals change, and change significantly. We may begin to prize depth over abundance, humility over arrogance, wisdom over knowledge, growth over comfort, and meaning over peace of mind. Then we begin to accept that we are the meaning-seeking, value-creating animal—matter charged with anima—and that death is an achievement of this life journey. From this perplexing engagement with mystery *soul* arises. Any flight from this soul-task leads us to naive delusion, distractions, immaturity, and superficiality. If we shrink from our deaths, we shrink from our lives. Again, Jung cautions us:

---

* With today's further extension of life, we might even describe this time as our third third, or fourth fourth. Soon we will surely reach and embody Shakespeare's famous "seven ages of man."

Natural life is the nourishing soil of the soul. Anyone who fails to go along with life remains suspended, stiff and rigid in midair. That is why so many people get wooden in old age; they look back and cling to the past with a secret fear of death in their hearts . . . but no living relationship to the present. From the middle of life onward, only he remains vitally alive who is ready to *die with life.**

Dying *with life* is clearly an oxymoron—to the ego, that is. In reality this living, sentient being who speaks to you, and you to whom I speak, are together always in mutual dying in the midst of life. So much social aggrandizement, political posturing, anesthetizing, projecting onto our children and cultural surrogates, flights into fantasies of immortality, take us further and further from ourselves, from the fundamental mystery of being itself, and the imperious question: Why are we here? Any theory about what comes after is only that—theory, or more commonly, the ratification of individual or tribal, angst-driven complexes.

While I intend no disrespect whatsoever to the affirmations of faith in an afterlife, I do ask that we simply not consider it a closed question, and therefore avoid the great depth, and complexity, to which our life always summons us. On the one hand we have a long cultural history of belief in an afterlife, and on the other hand we have the equally fervent denial of its existence by many others. But there is a middle ground here, one that respects and tolerates mystery and also honors the symbolic images that

* Jung, "The Soul and Death," *op. cit.*, par. 800.

emerge autonomously from our psyche. Jung seeks that middle ground:

> At some time someone is supposed to have invented a God and sundry dogmas and to have led humanity around by the nose with the "wish-fulfilling" fantasy.
>
> But this opinion is contradicted by the psychological fact that the head is a particularly inadequate organ when it comes to thinking up religious symbols. They do not come from the head at all, but from some other place, perhaps the heart; certainly from a deep psychic level very little resembling consciousness. . . . That is why religious symbols have a distinctly "revelatory" character. . . . They are anything rather than thought up; on the contrary, they have developed, plant-like, as natural manifestations of the human psyche.*

This middle ground asks that we respect symbol formations that are so clearly and universally represented in our psychological life, without necessarily converting them into presumptive metaphysical or eschatological "certainties." We need to be able to distinguish psychological truths from empirical truths, and both of them from personal complexes, but also to recognize that the symbols of the psyche, or soul, are in fact empirical realities as well.

The study of "the objective psyche" shows that the symbols of death and rebirth emerge time after time, culture after culture, aeon after aeon, and therefore must represent something fundamental to our psychological reality, something

---

* *Ibid.* par. 805.

that runs much deeper than wish fulfillment and projection.* After we have examined—and perhaps confessed our infantile desires for ego-consciousness continuance—the persistence of the forms and expressions of the archetype of rebirth or an afterlife must still be respected. As Jung explains:

> Experience shows that religions are in no sense conscious constructions, but that they arise from the natural life of the unconscious psyche and somehow give adequate expression to it. This explains their universal distribution and their enormous influence on humanity throughout history, which would be incomprehensible if religious symbols were not at the very least truths of man's psychological nature.**

After all, *we* do not create these symbols consciously, any more than we create our dreams, but *they are creating us!* All of this is profoundly mysterious, both threatening *and* intriguing to the tiny ego identification we call "ourselves." Such an encounter with transcendent energies, and within ourselves as well, is threatening because it challenges the ego's fantasy of sovereignty—"I am, who I think, feel, believe I am." But it is also intriguing because it relocates that ego in the context of a larger reality, the numinous realm we

---

* The Gnostic tradition affirmed the *Pleroma* as the fullness of divinity, the ground of being itself, with the *Archons* as the elemental powers that manifest and govern it, one of whom was Yahweh, among many others. This vision is not unlike the idea of the Collective Unconscious, which manifests in the world through archetypal expressions, including the gods, and the multiplicitous forms and motions of our daily lives. These dynamic forms move us through the biological, social, and spiritual courses of personal lives and collective histories.

** Jung, "The Soul and Death," *op. cit.,* par. 805.

have historically considered divinity. Jung once defined a neurosis as "a neglected god," meaning a failed relationship to this mystery, to these archetypal forms. While some will consider an open-ended mystery intriguing, others will find it fearful and will run back to fear-driven "certainties" and consensual validation from their huddled cohorts. So let them meet, vote on what is real, and live their lives accordingly. But the mystery remains, and will have its way with us, whatever our mechanisms of denial or ratified fears.

Wherever fear-driven formulations occur we may be sure that reality will sooner or later hold the trump card. As the poet Robert Frost once wrote, we sit in a circle and suppose, while the secret sits in the center and knows. Some of us will be able to tolerate ambiguity and be enlarged by an exploration of ever-deeper layers of mystery. Some will be driven to "certainties." But in the end, our lives will be governed by mysteries, not certainties. In the end, whatever is larger than our constructs and beliefs and denials will prove most worthy of our respect, our humility, and our considered beliefs. This is the experience of meaning. If we want our lives to be meaningful, we need to understand that meaning will not be found through any arrival at certainty, for any place we settle will soon prove inadequate. Meaning will arise from sundry departures from certainties, obligatory deaths and rebirths, and surprising new arrivals from which, then, new departures perforce persist. *This* is meaning.

In his fine book *Freud's Requiem*, Matthew von Unwerth recounts an incident in which Freud was accompanied by psychoanalyst and certified "character" Lou Andreas-Salomé and the poet Rainer Maria Rilke during a walk amid gorgeous summer flowers. Both Andreas-Salomé and Rilke reported that they could not enjoy the beauty of the flowers because they were so acutely aware of their evanescence—they knew that in moments the flowers would wither, and the observers pass also. Freud was stirred by this protestation against death to observe—there and in an essay that followed entitled "On Transience"—that we can never experience joy unless we also accept loss. The precondition of joy is to accept the gift of the moment, while knowing that it is only of the moment. Accordingly, we are led reluctantly to understand that the great threat of mortality is also its gift to us, for it not only differentiates the trivial from the lasting, but it summons us to ponder what really does matter to us.

Unwerth further notes that when Freud suffered his throat cancer, presumably from his many cigars, he chose not to give up smoking, knowing that his death was perhaps likely hastened. While we may, from a distance, moralize as much as we wish about the choice Freud made, is it not possible that we are only confessing our own neuroses around the matter and are threatened by Freud's decision? As Unwerth concludes, "However foolhardy it appears in hindsight, Freud's decision to continue smoking must have seemed to him a logical outgrowth of his conviction that life's value is not a pure calculation, but an essential personal choice. For Freud, it was the ability to enjoy life through love and work that determined its value. He was resolved to live to the fullest of his capacities—no matter the cost."*

Lest we think Freud narcissistic, or escapist, let us remember that this is a man who endured multiple radiations,

* Unwerth, *Freud's Requiem: Mourning, Memory, and the Invisible History of a Summer Walk*, p. 167.

multiple surgeries, a metal prosthesis of the palate, and refused even an aspirin lest it cloud his mind. This is a man I
admire, even as I would contend with some of his theories. I
also admire those who, with courage, choose to live their life,
or end it, in service to values that truly matter to them. For us
to judge their choices under the guise of morality, or sentimentality, is perhaps to confuse our fears with their resolve.

◆ ◆ ◆

Thus, the question of mortality and its meaning to us remains
open, and needs to. On the one hand, it has been my clinical
experience, and that of Jung and many other clinicians, that
the psyche does not grant a great deal of energy to death. Oh
yes, many people have death images in their dreams, and often
worry that such images presage their own imminent demise.
But I have never known that to be the case. The first dream
brought in by a forty-year-old analysand was, "I am in a hospital bed, and my favorite aunt Bernice enters and says to me,
'Julianne, it is time to die.' 'Oh, all right,' I say." This aunt was
Julianne's favorite, most supportive relative, and she trusted
the woman in her outer life, which is perhaps why the psyche
chose her to represent a trustworthy figure bringing a message
from the inner life. At forty, Julianne was ending a first half of
life history governed essentially by roles—mother, spouse,
homemaker—and was being summoned to a different journey
to develop other aspects of her personality. Her ego feared
that death, understandably, but from whence did her dream
come? It was the psyche's way of saying that it was time to die
unto the useful but already achieved, and perhaps exhausted,
identity and move to a new one. We do not get there—the

new, larger place—without dying to the old. "Unless ye die, ye shall not live."

On the other hand, those who are overtly dying typically have journey dreams, crossing dreams. We know well what the ego thinks about dying—it has an "attytood." But what does the psyche say? Jung observes:

> I was astonished to see how little ado the unconscious psyche makes of death. It would seem as though death were something relatively unimportant, or perhaps our psyche does not bother about what happens to the individual. But it seems that the unconscious is all the time interested in how one dies; that is, whether the attitude of consciousness is adjusted to dying or not.*

Clearly the psyche is not perturbed by death per se, at least not in the way that the conscious ego is. It may well be that nature is not interested in us after we have served whatever functions have been assigned to us. It is also possible to speculate that the psyche, or soul, persists in some fashion long after the ego life has ended. Whatever we consciously think about this matter, as I indicated before, is essentially irrelevant. What is relevant is what nature "thinks," what the psyche "thinks," and how we choose to live this short space allotted us in the meantime.

We think of death as the great antagonist, the Other who threatens us, forgetting all the while that death is our daily companion, not only in our existentially precarious perch above an abyss of annihilation, but in the sundry

* *Ibid.* par. 809.

deaths of daily concourse. Our cells are dying; our understandings are dying; even memory dies if we live long enough, but something abides, and something is served by this dying, even though the ego is not thrilled. (As the great American philosopher Woody Allen once observed, he was not afraid of dying; he just did not want to be there when it happened.)

But apart from these sundry deaths, there is a more insidious death, the death that comes through absenting ourselves from life, avoiding these mysteries. Death is only one way of dying; living partially, living fearfully, is our more common, daily collusion with death. As Jung asserted, "deviation from the truths of the blood beget neurotic restlessness. . . . Restlessness begets meaninglessness, and the lack of meaning in life is a soul-sickness."* Thus, a flight from the truth of our blood, which longs to return to the sea from whence we came, is a flight into the pseudo-world of illusion, distraction, and diminishment.

So our question is really less about death and more about how we are living, and what resolved values we embody in the face of mortality. Recalling Tithonus, life is meaningful precisely because it is finite—choices must be made, choices matter, and choices define the quality and character of our being here. To avoid, or to despair, is easy. Death is easy; life is hard. (This is a variant on the old theatrical maxim that "Death is easy, but comedy is hard." Whoever first said that, in my view, was vitally alive—joking, but alive.)** The ques-

---

* *Ibid*. par. 815.

** Variously ascribed to Sir Donald Wolfit, Miguel de Cervantes, Edmund Booth, and a host of others who no doubt wished they had said this.

tion is not how to solve our mortal condition; that is hubris and delusion. The question rather is: How to live? Paradoxically, mortality, our most unwelcome guest, is a friend, for it requires that question of us, the addressing of which brings us whatever quality we can manage in this short, precious life.

After he had nearly died from a heart attack, Jung wrote of his experience to his friend Kristine Mann:

> My illness proved to be a most valuable experience, which gave me the inestimable opportunity of a glimpse behind the veil. The only difficulty is to get rid of the body, to get quite naked and void of the world and the ego-will. When you can give up the crazy will to live and when you seemingly fall into a bottomless mist, then the truly *real* life begins with everything which you were meant to be and never reached. It is something ineffably grand. I was free, completely free and whole, as I never felt before.*

Approaching such mystery with an open heart is what paradoxically makes this life richer. Before concluding where we may or may not be going, it might be more productive to be sure first that we are here.

---

* Jung, *Letters I*, p. 357.

Chapter Thirteen

THAT WE ACCEPT AT LAST THAT OUR HOME IS OUR JOURNEY, AND OUR JOURNEY IS OUR HOME

"One never reaches home. But where paths that have an affinity for each other intersect, the whole world looks like home for a time."
HERMANN HESSE, *DEMIAN*

"The lord whose oracle is in Delphi neither speaks nor conceals but gives a sign."
HERACLITUS, *FRAGMENTS*

". . . no churches where God
is imprisoned and lamented
like a trapped animal . . .
no yearning for an afterlife . . .
but only longing for what belongs to us.
RAINER MARIA RILKE, *DAS STUNDENBUCH*

*O*ur histories embody a paradox that humming beneath all of our lives is a strange rhythm of *exile* and *homecoming*. Recall that our birth is an ejection from a secure linkage to a nurturant cosmos into a perilous world in which we are beset with painful opposites and driven by powers indifferent to our well-being. If we do not render our exile conscious, we burden our partners with inordinate expectations; we are prone to lives of distraction or superficiality; and we adopt beliefs that offend reason and daily experience in service to the comfort of facile promises—whether political, social, economic, or theological—that ultimately leave us dissatisfied and anxious. So before we consider the question of home and homecoming, we have to consider how and why exile is necessary—necessary for growth, empowering experience, and individuation.

◆ ◆ ◆

The developmental process that leads to our growth, maturation, and fuller personhood is a continuing *vocatus*, namely, "a call." Rising from deep within us, the call comes to change—to die unto the old understanding and adaptations, the old comforts and compromises—and when we resist the call of our psyche we grow sicker and sicker, or more and more depressed, and have to work harder just to stay in place. Accepting the necessity of exile is to also accept the possibility of homecoming. As Hesse's *Steppenwolf* expressed it, "We have to stumble through so much dirt and humbug before we reach home. And we have no one to guide us. Our only guide is our homesickness."*

But let us also consider the following stages of our common developmental journey: call, exile, and homecoming.

1. *One is called to the next stage, to a task.* The task may be to learn to thrive without the protection of another, to cope with

* Hesse, *Steppenwolf*, p. 153.

divorce or loss, to manage self-esteem in the face of defeats and disappointments. Such passages always require that we depart from what we have known, perhaps treasured, perhaps loathed, perhaps feared, and move to the next place, whether the imperative comes from our social environment, which asks responsibility of us, or from the changes in our body, which pay no heed to our resistance, or from a deep spiritual hunger that calls us to new venues. This "call" may not come as an angelic message in a dream, but can manifest as symptomatology: boredom, panic, burnout, depression, or desuetude. This "call" is engineered by the psyche, although the ego, which comprehends only conventional discourse, may not recognize these cryptic messengers from below.*

As an old parable has it, a king sent us to this strange land with a task. We arrived some time ago, forgot or were intimidated by the assignment, and now wander around in noise and confusion along with others who have similarly forgotten that they were given a task, and that we all were sent by a king.

2. *The task that each of us is to address is different,* although collectively we may call the task *individuation,* the summons to individual personhood. Our gift to the world will be that separate piece we bring to the whole, but how difficult that assignment often proves. Tiny, vulnerable as we all are, we adapt, take on the coloration of our environment, and soon lose the linkage to what we think, or feel, or desire, or *what wants to come into the world through us.*

3. *Such tasks pull us out of our comfort zones.* Once we leave the protective space one associates with "home," one is alone,

---

* Knowing the difference between *signs* and *symbols,* between literal problems demanding literal solutions, and discerning that one is really being invited to a deeper dialogue, too often lies outside the province of conventional behavioral, cognitive, or pharmacological therapy, and is the reason why depth therapy, psychodynamic therapy, exists.

even more vulnerable, and desperately in need of consensual validation. It is scary out there alone, on the edge of our being, and we pull back and hang on to the platform before springing into the depths. When Nietzsche said that *we* are an abyss, he had it right. But he added that we are also the tightrope across that abyss, though we fear risking ourselves in those in scary in-betweens.

4. *We risk inflation in these moments*, as much as intimidation. Inflation means that one is caught up in a hubristic complex without the balancing, without the consideration of the opposite that prevents us from overconfidence, rashness, or refusal to consider competing values. (I recall an analyst in Zürich who dreamt that he was flying over Zürich [without an airplane] and the voice of God said to him that he was "called to correct Jung." Well, there is much in Jung that calls out for correction, or at least reconsideration, as Jung himself would quickly concur,* but this person went on to separate himself from colleagues and fly off to set up his own narcissistically driven operation, rather than stay behind and dialogue honestly with areas of disagreement.)

5. As the fairy tales, or *Märchen* ("the stories," as they are called in German), tell us, the kingdom is ill because *some value has been lost, neglected, repressed, or forgotten*. In the course of the story, which dramatizes how our intrapsychic components are in disarray, healing occurs not from the powers on high, associated with conscious ego understandings, but from the lowly, neglected, or marginalized—the dwarf, the helpful animal, the wee folk. Sometimes the missing queen suggests that a "feminine" value has been repressed. Sometimes the aridity

---

* Jung famously observed that he was "Jung, thank God, and not a Jungian."

of the land bespeaks a depression wherein linkage to the spirit has been severed. Sometimes the character is "bewitched," which is to say, has fallen under the spell of an immobilizing complex. What these repeated motifs tell us is that much of our summons forth into the world involves redeeming a value that has been lost or repudiated through the adaptations required by our environment. Such a value must be revisited, integrated, lived, in order to bring healing to the kingdom or trigger the next stage in our personal development toward wholeness.

6.   *Flight from this restorative task, as well as the honest experience of exile, will bring the retribution of "the gods."* In masking our symptoms, in running from our developmental task, we thwart the will of forces larger than our conscious understanding. What is denied of the gods will always oblige them to reassert their imperative in forceful terms. Recall that a neurosis is "a neglected god," meaning that some profound energy or value has been repressed, pathologized, and is now reasserting its will upon us. Expressed in concrete terms, whenever we force ourselves to do what is against our nature's intent, we will suffer anxiety attacks, depressions, or addictions to anesthetize the pain of this inner dislocation. We can run, but we cannot escape the laws of our own nature.

7.   *The pathology that arises from any flight from the task is necessary to get our attention. Psychopathology* literally means "the expression of the suffering of the soul." We should not pathologize *pathology* but rather see it as the autonomous response of the psyche to our choices and priorities, an autonomous refusal to cooperate in further self-alienation. Pathology is what brings one to Twelve Step groups, to therapy, to confession, to reconciliation with others and potentially with oneself.

Pathology has to hurt enough to call us back to our task, to recognize the wrong turn, and to get on a different road. Pathology is our friend, though few of us are quite willing to consider it so at the time.

8. *Suffering is the requisite for consciousness and recovery.* None of us welcomes suffering; we wish to rescue ourselves from it as quickly as possible—with medication, with distraction, with trivialization, with denial. But suffering is always humbling. Humbling always brings us back to ourselves, for no one can live it for us or remove it from us. In each visitation to these surly savannas of suffering, there is a task, the addressing of which will lead us to enlargement rather than diminishment, even when our outer freedoms have been constricted. Suffering will typically prove the catalyst, or at least the opening, to recover the journey, to return to the task of homecoming.

9. *Homecoming is the goal, but our "home" is not "out there," a geographic place, the protective "other," or a comforting theology or psychology.* "Homecoming" means returning to a relationship with the Self, a relationship that was there in the beginning, but from which we necessarily strayed in our obligatory adaptations to the explicit and implicit demands of family, tribe, and culture. Homecoming means healing, means integration of the split-off parts of the soul, means redeeming the dignity and high purpose of our soul's journey. When we are here to live our soul's journey, we can spontaneously be generous to others, for we have much to give from our inner abundance; we can draw and maintain boundaries, for we have learned the difference between their journey and ours; and we can sort through different value clashes because we have found a personal authority that helps us discern what is authentic for

us. In short, we have recovered a relationship to the soul (psyche) from which we lost contact, but that nonetheless continues to hum beneath the surface of our lives and never, ever loses contact with us.

We learn the truth of T. S. Eliot's lines that the end of all our journeys is to arrive at the beginning and to know it for the first time.

◆ ◆ ◆

Having lived for many years a few miles from the casinos of Atlantic City, I grew to despise them. Intuiting that the splashy money guys—the ones who promised to rebuild the sad city, whose gaming tables would employ the unemployed—had arrived in the Garden State out of their own interests and not that of others, I voted against the legislation that legitimized the casinos in the 1970s. In later years, I learned too much about how the casinos really worked, how skilled personnel immigrated to the area to supplant the local unemployed, how millions were skimmed off and sent elsewhere, and how many sad stories of the ruination of simple people were not covered in the media. Moreover, many employees whose souls were sucked out of them became my patients and confessed what it was really like to work in those gaudy pleasure pits.

I recount these sad and sordid facts to indicate how surprising it was that years later, one of my greatest epiphanies occurred when I was in a casino. My wife and I had made very few forays to the casinos over the years. We did take various visiting relatives or friends on anthropological visits; we did go to see Harry Belafonte (twice), Liza Minnelli, and Sammy Davis, Jr. But on one occasion, we were given tickets by a friend for a variety show. As it turned out, the tickets were for the front row, stage center. Naively, I thought that was the surprise of the evening. The show wound on, with singers, comedians, and then two acrobats from Mexico who asked for a volunteer. Naturally, no one in his right mind would volunteer. So they went into the audience and dragged a poor schlub onto the stage. To not have gone with them would have meant that, literally, he would have had to slug them, and he was too polite to do that.

So, this poor schlub, aka *moi*, was suddenly center stage, in a spotlight, facing perhaps six hundred strangers. It would be wrong to say that I suffered stage fright, but I did experience an altered state, simply from the surreality of it all. They asked my name, and I responded. Then they asked where I was from, and at that moment, my history began a slow crawl on an inner teleprompter wherein I revisited all the places I had lived. Although only milliseconds were transpiring, it seemed as if time had stopped in my disassociated state. In those milliseconds I wanted to say "Zürich," where I had undertaken a lengthy analysis, gone through life and death, and entered a different stage of life. "No," I thought, "that is a metaphor, not a place, and they will not understand that."

By this time the two acrobats thought they had pulled the world's biggest dummy on stage and one of them said, "Oh, asked too tough a question for you?" "Linwood, New Jersey," I said. Whereupon, he said, "Let's hear it for Linwood, New Jersey!" By this time the out-of-towners, the drunks, the ladies in purple hair, and the waitstaff had gotten a good laugh at the dumbstruck schlub. Things went downhill from there as I participated in their acrobatic acts and nearly got killed, but after the show when we walked out, someone said, "You were part of the act, weren't you?" "No," I said, "we just came to watch the show." I could tell that he did not believe me, rubbing shoulders as he was with such genuine showbiz talent as I was—that is, so talented at playing the schlub that in fact I was.

On the drive home we reflected on the bizzare evening. All we wanted to do was go out, relax, and visit a different world. And so we did. In that moment of surreality I had seen through the thin cerements that this world wears to behold some deeper form within. When I asked myself why I wanted to say "Zürich," rather than a town in New Jersey, I realized that the traumatic occasion had thrust me into the inner world and that I had phenomenologically experienced the truth, namely, that *our journey is our home*, not the locale where we carry out our life.

I am not suggesting that place is unimportant. We need to consider whether the locale, nature, culture, climate, all of the above and more, support or impede our lives. (A distant colleague once said that where I have lived and worked this past decade, Houston, was uninhabitable for her, for the above reasons. It has been most habitable for me because it is a place where I am able to live my journey, perhaps fuller than ever before.) In referring to Zürich, I was not referring to a place, of course, but rather to a process, a moment of meeting one's appointment with destiny. I think we all have appointments to keep, appointments with others to be sure, but most of all, appointments with the meaning of our journey—why we are here, why we are sucking air, and whether we are adding to or subtracting from the world. And many people, I have noticed, do not show up for their appointments. When they do not, whose life are they living? Where did they get off the path meant for them by the gods?

We all get off the path for a while because we are tiny, dependent, ignorant, afraid, and thus the second half of life, if we are granted one by fate, is about getting back on the path, our path, whether approved by parents, endorsed by a consensus of our tribe, or comforting or not.

A number of years ago I read a book by Peter Matthiessen called *The Snow Leopard.* It is an eloquent, personally revealing, first-person account of his hitting a very rough patch in his life, his sense of inner desperation, and his soul's summons to risk a "silly" passion to at least know that he was still alive. He decides that he will journey to the Himalaya Mountains of Tibet in search of a snow leopard, that rare, rich, beautiful beast that roams those altitudes and has a certain mystical cachet as a result. He went, as Sir Edmund Hillary said of climbing Everest, "because it was there." A wonderful, foolish, and risky passion.

After a long and perilous journey requiring great discipline, suffering, and hardship, hearing reports of sightings here and there, tracking the elusive creature, missing him by hours, he finally returns. When asked by others, "Did you see the snow leopard?" he replies, "No—isn't that wonderful?"

Only a person who has truly been on the road can say of such a "failure," "No, isn't that wonderful?" By then, he had learned that the task is not to find the object* but to live the journey, with passion, and risk, and commitment, and danger. It has nothing to do, per se, with the seductions of exotic soil, or success, or arrival. For some of us, the risk of loving another in the face of our forbidding history provides our journey. For others, risking a talent, an enthusiasm, an imaginative summons, is our journey. What if Matthiessen had seen the snow leopard? Whatever that exhilaration, it would be but a moment, and then the task of quotidian life would return. Rather, the shimmering image of the elusive gave him his journey, and gave him almost unbearable richness as well.

◆ ◆ ◆

So, what has my journey been about? Perhaps it might be summarized, and it is only a summary of a very complex matter, as a search for *God*. As a young person, I must have thought He or She was an object (perhaps hiding in South Dakota, or Curaçao, or Paraguay), and if I looked long enough in enough places, I would find that missing object. Most of my searching was, admittedly, in books on the subject, as you can imagine. Such naïveté is embarrassing today, but reflects our ego's common tendency to literalize mystery in service to its own needs for clarity, order, predictability.

"So," some reader will ask, "did you ever find Him or Her?" "No," I will say, "isn't that wonderful?" Any god I

---

* As *object* only, the thing sought will in the end disappoint, prove partial, prove inadequate to the magnitude of the soul—as our materialistic obsessions have revealed to us over and over again. If objects made us happy, or fulfilled, or connected us to transcendent energies, then we would truly be the richest people in history instead of possibly the most spiritually impoverished.

would have "found" would have proved a mere artifact of my limited understanding at the moment, a temporary construct of my poor brain and constitutionally constricted imagination. As Lao-Tse said, "The Tao that can be named is not the Tao." As Kierkegaard said, "The god that can be named is not God." As Tillich said, "God is the God that appears out from behind the god that has disappeared." Any God I would have "found" would have become an object, a noun, and not God the verb, an idol constructed by my limited consciousness, not a transcendent, transforming energy.

Dante ends *La Commedia* by praising the love that moves the Heavens and the Earth. My son Timothy sent me a poem via e-mail titled "Wild Energy," in which his sentence puts it perfectly:

> *There is something larger than self, that we either mangle or make significant.*

I have sought to respect that mystery always. Learning to live with ambiguity is learning to live with how life really is, full of complexities and strange surprises, for as Voltaire observed, "Doubt is not a pleasant condition, but certainty is certainly absurd." Spare us from those who are "certain," for their certainties will become tomorrow's institutionalized tyrannies—for them, and for the rest of us. Recall also Gotthold Lessing's aphorism in the eighteenth century that if God were to hold in his right hand the truth and in his left hand the search for truth, one should choose the left, "truth" being accessible only to divinity, but the journey toward it, ever toward it, our noblest, most faithful calling. As Jung observed, "The phenomenology of the psyche is so colorful, so variegated in form and meaning, that we cannot possibly reflect all its riches in one mirror. Nor in our description of it can we ever embrace the whole, but must be content to shed light only on single parts of the total phenomenon."*

How presumptive I once was, and so many theologians remain, to think that one could encompass the magnitude of mystery, or subsume the putative contradictions that vex our ego into reassuring dogmas. As Hesse's character Steppenwolf puts it, "It is hard to find this track of the divine in the midst of this life we lead, in this besotted humdrum age of spiritual blindness,"** yet that mission is our most profound calling. If the Tao that is named is not the Tao, then anything my puny mental and imaginative apparatus apprehends is surely not worthy of the appellation of *divinity.* So, as philosopher Ludwig Wittgenstein cautions, "Whereof one cannot speak, thereof one must remain silent."

Accordingly, I am so happy now with the ambiguity that would have oppressed my soul in earlier days. I can live with the ambiguity that tortured me as a young person, and that still drives so many of my coevals to fundamentalism. In the nineteenth century, poet John Keats praised the capacity for "negative capability" in a letter, namely, holding the tension of opposites without an anxious grasping for certainty. Finding "God" would have been a death, although I could not have known that then. Such a "God" would have been an artifact of the moment, not the energy that drives the universe and drives each of us in transcendent aspiration. Finding such a "God" would have meant an arrival, and all

---

* Jung, *CW 15*, "Introduction to 'Psychology and Literature,' " Par. 2.

** Hesse, *op.cit.*, p. 30.

arrivals become, in time, places of constriction, from which one perforce must leave or die.

Yes, the faithful will say, "So much for your folly; I have found my God." And I say, "Good for you, and has that God brought you into greater depth, more complexity, more mystery? Or has that God brought you the stultification that we confuse with peace?" "But my God," they may say, "is the true God, and you are full of ignorance and delusion." And I will reply, "I will abide my ignorance and delusion, knowing it is such, and can you be as honest?" And they will say, "You are the bitter fruit of modern education and psychology, and, thus, atheism." And I would say that I would never choose a posture as ignorant as atheism, knowing what I have experienced of the energies within myself and in the rich world around me. And I would add, "I have found intimations of the divine in the heart, in what Blake called the sacred imagination, in moments of grace and intertwined thighs with the beloved, and in the mystery of death and rebirth. Moreover, one moment of music from Beethoven, one painting by Hundertwasser or Klee, one lyric of Rilke, has given me more access to the divine than all the hortatory sermons I've ever heard." And they will say that I am hopeless, and I will say that I am filled with hope, remembering Eliot's admonition to beware of what we hope for, cautioning that we not "hope, for hope would be hope for the wrong thing." I am filled with hope that around the next corner, the new and the unexpected will cause me to reinvent myself, revise my way of seeing, and take me back to the point of beginning, which is awe, which is wonder, which is curiosity, which is terror, and which is perduring summons to stay in the fight. Through all, as Plotinus observed in *The*

Enneads, "the world is full of signs, and the wise will begin to see them."

◆ ◆ ◆

As we have seen, the agenda of the first half of life is forged from suffering demands of all kinds and responding to the blows, challenges, and seductions of life, while the second half of life has more to do with wrestling with the aftermath: guilt, anger, recrimination, regret, recovery, and the possibility of forgiveness of self and others. The former is one kind of struggle—mostly with the world—and the latter is mostly with ourselves and the questions of transcendent meaning that continue to perturb us. The Greek novelist Nikos Kazantzakis reported questioning a monk in a monastery whether he still wrestled with the Devil every day. The elderly monk replied that he had pretty much fought with the Devil every day during his youth, but that the two of them had gotten tired of fighting each other. But presently, the monk said, he found he was fighting most with God.*

How much courage will we find to stay in the fight and be honest with ourselves at the same time? Novelist Peter De Vries put it in terms that will be terrifying to most readers, yet I find he is being honest with himself, with us, and clearly staying in the fight. He walks out of the comfort zone and risks being really, really honest with himself. He expresses it in this way:

---

* One is reminded of Yeats's account of his struggle: "Now his wars on God begin. / At stroke of midnight God shall win."

I believe that man must learn to live without those consolations called religions, which his own intelligence must by now have told him belong to the childhood of the race. Philosophy can really give us nothing permanent to believe either; it is too rich in answers, each canceling out the rest. The quest for Meaning is foredoomed. Human life "means" nothing. But that is not to say that life is not worth living. What does a Debussy *Arabesque* "mean," or a rainbow or a rose? A man delights in all of these, knowing himself to be no more—a wisp of music and a haze of dreams dissolving against the sun. Man has only his two feet to stand on, his own human trinity to see him through: Reason, Courage, and Grace. And the first plus the second equals the third.*

While I might cavil a bit, and ask why that particular music, that phenomenon of nature touches and stirs us if it does not bear some resemblance to something within us, I respect and am humbled by his integrity. Such resonance as De Vries describes also suggests to me that we are related to something truly outside ourselves. Regrettably, what we call institutional "religion" has too often been a defense of personal neuroses, a ratification of troubling complexes and burgeoning bureaucracies, but it is also true that sometimes religion brings out the best in us . . . sometimes. (But just as often not, since more atrocities have been perpetrated in the name of religion than in the name of politics. Surely, we have always to remember what the great Spanish painter Goya etched into an engraving: "The sleep of rea-

* Peter De Vries, *The Blood of the Lamb*, pp. 166–67.

son produces monsters.") Still, I admire De Vries's journey and believe that his reason and courage brought him to a spiritual place both right for him and consistent with his experience.

Finally, it may prove true that carrying on this troubled journey in the face of doubt, defeat, and the imminence of death is either damn foolish or the noblest gift of the spirit. To recognize our finitude, the fragility of our fictions, the humbling of our hubris, is intimidating and demoralizing, yet . . . yet, therein lies the path toward the construction of "meaning" that De Vries denied.

We are moments only, at best, and then gone. If one thinks there is a better place elsewhere that justifies all the lunacy on this earth, then fine. That will take care of itself, then, won't it? Right now, here, is where we live, and what are we to do with it? How are we to live *here* and experience this high summons to be the agents of the meaning of our lives? How can we walk that fine line between acknowledging our emptiness and fraudulence, and the grandeur and heroism with which we continue the journey? On the one hand, as Scott Fitzgerald's character Dick Diver reminds us, "The strongest guard is placed at the gateway to nothing. . . . Maybe because the condition of emptiness is too shameful to be divulged."* And on the other hand, in our seemingly provincial ways, we are also carrying the vast project of evolutionary history forward.

Still, another novelist, Mark Helprin, offers a middle path, both heroic and humbling, enervating but engaging, enlarging:

---

* Fitzgerald, *Tender Is the Night*, p. 70.

. . . you learn early, that love can overcome death, and that what is required of you in this is memory and devotion. Memory and devotion. To keep your love alive you must be willing to be obstinate, and irrational, and true, to fashion your entire life as a construct, a metaphor, a fiction, a device for the exercise of faith. Without this, you will live like a beast and have nothing but an aching heart. With it, your heart, though broken, will be full, and you will stay in the fight until the very last.*

Similarly, a character in Thomas Bernhard's *Old Masters* explains his passion for the journey. "There is no perfect picture and there is no perfect book and there is no perfect piece of music . . . that is the truth, and this truth makes it possible for a mind like mine, which all its life was nothing but a desperate mind, to go on existing. One's mind has to be a searching mind, a mind searching for mistakes, for the mistakes of humanity, a mind searching for failure. The human mind is only a human mind when it searches for the mistakes of humanity. . . . A good mind is a mind that searches for the mistakes of humanity and an exceptional mind is a mind which finds these mistakes of humanity, and a genius's mind is a mind which, having found these mistakes, points them out. . . ."** From such passion, such magnificent "failures," we add to the sum of things learned, our human topography gets even more interesting, and our traveler's sensibility grows still more observant, still more vigilant along the journey.

---

* Mark Helprin, *Memoir from Antproof Case*, p. 514.

** Bernhard, *Old Masters: A Comedy*, p. 20.

In his novel *Demian*, Hermann Hesse writes that in a world of travelers, when paths intersect, the world seems like home for a while. All of us are travelers, and there is a sweet, centripetal accord, a rapprochement when we meet, touch, converse with each other, and then, and then . . . our journey returns, and we resume the challenge of our centrifugal journeys outward, past the far-flung tangents of our ancestors to regions as yet only dreamed in our unconscious, across the oceanic universe in which we daily swim.

The modern Greek poet Cavafy imagines Odysseus toward the end of his journey. Remember the odyssey we all began: Summoned as youngish persons to a foolish adventure, bloodied by life as we all are, sooner or later we yearn to come home, wherever it may be. Thus, Odysseus is our archetypal comrade. In a poem titled "Ithaca," the home toward which Odysseus persists, Cavafy wonders what the storm-tossed mariner might think when his battered barque pulls at last into the harbor. Will this village of mud huts, these people who scarcely know him after twenty years, really prove "home" when one has been thrust upon the wine-dark sea for so long? Will it be possible for such a voyager to settle into an easy chair, open a six-pack, and watch the ball game the rest of his life? Cavafy concludes with this unbidden advice to the mariner that "Ithaca" was never the goal, really; rather Ithaca's gift was to give him his journey, with all its painful richness, from which, "you must surely have understood by then what Ithacas mean."* What gives us our journey also gives us our home, our richness, our meaning.

As Alfred North Whitehead reminded us, "It is the

---

* C. P. Cavafy, "Ithaca," *The Complete Poems of Cavafy*, p. 37.

business of the future to be dangerous." The challenge to each of us is to accept the danger of our personal journey and thereby accept the gift of our lives. Perhaps our further challenge, as now revealed in the private letters of Mother Teresa, is, with or without certainty, to find our good work in this world and do it faithfully.* In mindfully selecting our "useful fiction" to serve, we find what proves of inherent value to us, through which many blessings come to us in return.

◆   ◆   ◆

This search for God, this longing for meaning and understanding, while often frustrating, has given me my journey, and my journey has given me greater acquaintance with many gods along the way—all, especially the dark ones, worthy of and demanding respect—and many good and many bad people, but always *an interesting life.* In the end, having a more interesting life, a life that disturbs complacency, a life that pulls us out of the comfortable and thereby demands a larger spiritual engagement than we planned or that feels comfortable, is *what matters most.*

To have been here, to have wrestled with such things, to have lived such questions, to have kept the mystery before us, to have joyfully accepted being "defeated by ever-larger things," to have kept one's appointment with destiny, to have taken one's journey through this dark, bitter, luminous, wondrous universe, to have risked being who we really are, is, finally, *what matters most.*

---

* Mother Teresa's spiritual anguish amid her good work was earlier mirrored by Miguel de Unamuno in the novella titled *St. Emmanuel the Good, Martyr.*

BIBLIOGRAPHY

Achenbaum, Andrew. *Older Americans, Vital Communities: A Bold Vision for Societal Aging.* Baltimore: John Hopkins University Press, 2005.

Adcock, Fleur. *Poems: 1960–2000.* Newcastle: Bloodaxe Books. 2000.

Agee, James. *A Death in the Family.* New York: Bantam, 1957.

Allison, Alexander et. al., eds. *The Norton Anthology of Poetry.* New York: W. W. Norton and Co., 1983.

Arendt, Hannah. *Crises of the Republic.* New York: Harvest Books, 1972.

Augustine, St. *City of God.* New York: Penguin Classics, 2003.

Barfield, Owen. *Saving the Appearances: A Study in Idolatry.* London: Faber and Faber, 1957.

Bernhard, Thomas. *Old Masters: A Comedy.* Chicago: University of Chicago Press, 1992.

Bonhoeffer, Dietrich. *Letters and Papers from Prison.* New York: Macmillan, 1972.

Brant, Mary Jane Hurley. *When Every Day Matters: A Mother's Memoir on Love, Loss, and Life.* Washington, DC: Simple Abundance Press, 2008.

Cavafy, C. P. *The Complete Poems of Cavafy*. Trans. Rae Dalven. New York: Harcourt, Brace, and World, 1963.

De Vries, Peter. *The Blood of the Lamb*. Chicago: University of Chicago Press, 1961.

Dostoyevsky, Fyodor. *Notes from Underground*. New York: New American Library, 1961.

Dunn, Stephen. *Different Hours*. New York: W. W. Norton and Co., 2000.

Emerson, Ralph Waldo. *The Writings of Ralph Waldo Emerson*. New York: Modern Library, 1940.

Fitzgerald, F. Scott. *Tender Is the Night*. New York: Scribner, 1982.

Gilgamesh: A New English Version. Stephen Mitchell, trans. New York: Free Press, 2004.

Goldhagen, Daniel. *Hitler's Willing Executioners: Ordinary Germans and the Holocaust*. New York: Vintage, 1997.

Güggenbuhl-Craig, Adolf. *The Emptied Soul*. Putnam, CT: Spring Publications, 2004.

Haftmann, Werner. *The Mind and Work of Paul Klee*. New York: Frederick A. Praeger, 1967.

Helprin, Mark. *Memoir from Antproof Case*. New York: Avon Books, 1995.

Hemingway, Ernest. *The Sun Also Rises*. New York: Scribner, 1954.

Hesse, Hermann. *Steppenwolf*. New York: Henry Holt and Company, 1963.

Hollis, James. *The Archetypal Imagination*. College Station, TX: Texas A&M University Press, 2000.

———. *Creating a Life: Finding Your Individual Path*. Toronto: Inner City Books, 2001.

———. *The Eden Project: In Search of the Magical Other*. Toronto: Inner City Books, 1998.

———. *Finding Meaning in the Second Half of Life: How to Finally, Really Grow Up*. New York: Gotham Books/ Penguin, 2005.

———. *The Middle Passage: From Misery to Meaning at Mid-Life*. Toronto: Inner City Books, 1993.

———. *On This Journey We Call Our Life: Living the Questions*. Toronto: Inner City Books, 2003.

———. *Swamplands of the Soul: New Life in Dismal Places*. Toronto: Inner City Books, 1996.

———. *Tracking the Gods: The Place of Myth in Modern Life*. Toronto: Inner City Books, 1995.

———. *Why Good People Do Bad Things: Understanding Our Darker Selves*. New York: Gotham Books/Penguin, 2007.

Ibsen, Henrik. *Ghosts* in *A Doll's House and Other Plays*. New York: Penguin, 1965.

Jung, Carl Gustav. *The Collected Works*. Trans. R.F.C. Hull, Eds. H. Read, M. Fordham, G. Adler, W. McGuire. Princeton: Princeton University Press, 1973. [*The Collected Works* are abbreviated *CW* in this book.]

———. *Letters I-II 1906–1961*. Eds. Gerhard Adler, Aniela Jaffé. London: Routledge, 1973.

Matthiessen, Peter. *The Snow Leopard*. New York: Penguin Books, 1987.

Momaday, N. Scott and Al Momaday. *The Way to Rainy Mountain*. Tucson: University of Arizona Press, 1996.

Mathes, Charlotte. *And a Sword Shall Pierce Your Heart: Moving from Despair to Meaning After the Death of a Child*. Wilmette, IL: Chiron, 2006.

Pascal, Blaise. *Pensées*. New York: Dutton, 1958.

Recer, Paul. "Scientists Solve Firefly Mystery," *The Associated Press*, June 28, 2001.

Rilke, Rainer Maria. *Ahead of All Parting: The Selected Poetry and Prose of Rainer Maria Rilke*. Trans., Stephen Mitchell. New York: Modern Library, 1995.

Spong, John Shelby. *Jesus for the Non-Religious: Recovering the Divine at the Heart of the Human*. San Francisco: Harper-Collins, 2007.

The Norton Anthology of Poetry, Alexander Allison et al., eds. New York: W. W. Norton and Company, 1983.

Unwerth, Matthew von. *Freud's Requiem: Mourning, Memory, and the Invisible History of a Summer Walk*. New York: Riverhead Books, 2005.

von Franz, Marie-Louise. *The Problem of the Puer Aeternus*. Toronto: Inner City Books, 2000.

Yeats, William Butler. *Selected Poems and Two Plays*. Ed. M. L. Rosenthal, New York: Macmillan, 1962.

INDEX

Note Page numbers followed by an 'n' refer to notes at the end of the page.